Thomas Dunbar Ingram

Two Chapters of Irish History

Thomas Dunbar Ingram

Two Chapters of Irish History

ISBN/EAN: 9783744717144

Printed in Europe, USA, Canada, Australia, Japan

Cover: Foto ©ninafisch / pixelio.de

More available books at **www.hansebooks.com**

TWO CHAPTERS

OF

IRISH HISTORY

I. THE IRISH PARLIAMENT OF JAMES II

II. THE ALLEGED VIOLATION OF THE TREATY OF LIMERICK

BY

T. DUNBAR INGRAM, LL.D.

AUTHOR OF
'A HISTORY OF THE LEGISLATIVE UNION OF GREAT BRITAIN AND IRELAND'

"Irish policy is Irish history, and I have no faith in any statesman who attempts to remedy the evils of Ireland who is either ignorant of the past or who will not take lessons from it."—BEACONSFIELD.

London
MACMILLAN AND CO.
AND NEW YORK
1888

All rights reserved

CONTENTS

CHAPTER I

THE IRISH PARLIAMENT OF JAMES II

	PAGE
Section I. IRELAND FROM 1641 TO THE ACCESSION OF JAMES II	1
,, II. THE PREPARATION FOR THE PARLIAMENT	29
,, III. THE PARLIAMENT OF 1689	59

CHAPTER II

THE ALLEGED VIOLATION OF THE TREATY OF LIMERICK

Section I. THE SECOND SIEGE AND TREATY OF LIMERICK	93
,, II. THE CHARGE OF INTOLERANCE AGAINST THE IRISH PROTESTANT PARLIAMENT	124

APPENDIX

1. TWO COLUMNS OF NAMES FROM THE LIST OF PERSONS ATTAINTED BY THE IRISH PARLIAMENT	141
2. TREATY OF LIMERICK, AS RATIFIED BY THEIR MAJESTIES' LETTERS PATENT UNDER THE GREAT SEAL OF ENGLAND	143

CHAPTER I

THE IRISH PARLIAMENT OF JAMES II

SECTION I

IRELAND FROM 1641 TO THE ACCESSION OF JAMES II

THE forty years which immediately preceded the breaking out of the Rebellion of 1641 were the most peaceful and prosperous which Ireland had seen for centuries. The industrial progress of the island during this period was remarkable. For the first time in her history Ireland paid her way. The soil was greatly improved by applying to it modes of husbandry with which the native inhabitants had hitherto been unacquainted. New and profitable employments were introduced, manufactures were established. The linen manufacture in particular had made such an advance as to establish among our historians the mistaken idea that it was first introduced by Lord Strafford.[1] The value of lands and their rents had increased. In 1640 the customs amounted to almost four times the sum which was received from them at the commencement of the century. Shipping had increased a

---

[1] Long before Strafford was born linen cloth was manufactured in and exported from Ireland. To buy linen cloth, except in open fair, was punishable by the 33 Henry VIII, c. 2. By the 11 Eliz. c. 10 it was forbidden to export linen yarns without paying the enormous duty of twelvepence a pound. By the 13 Eliz. c. 1 it was provided that none but merchants inhabiting staple or corporate towns should export cloth made of linen yarn. The Rev. Charles O'Conor says, "The antiquity of linen cloth in Ireland is lost in the night of the remotest ages of our history."—*Historical Address*, pt. ii. p. 255.

hundredfold, commerce had extended, and the export trade was in the most satisfactory condition. Sir John Davis, writing in 1613, tells us in his quaint and figurative language that the strings of the Irish harp were all in tune and made a good harmony in the commonwealth: "So as we may well conceive a hope that Ireland . . . will from henceforth prove a land of peace and concord."[1]

But the strings of the Irish harp were not fated to be long in tune, or to give forth harmonious sounds. The growing prosperity of Ireland was shattered in a moment. Encouraged by the Scotch invasion of England, and by the successes which his revolted subjects had obtained over Charles I, the Irish wantonly threw away the blessings offered them by Providence. The rebellion broke out on the 22d of October 1641. At first it was purely anti-English. The northern rebels declared that "they would not leave an Englishman in the country; that they would have no English king, but one of their own nation, and Sir Phelim O'Neal should be their king; that neither the King nor Queen of England should govern Ireland any longer; that if they had His Majesty in their power they would flay him alive; that they would give a great sum of money to have his head," etc.[2] But Roger Moore persuaded the rebels to refrain from open threats against the English, and to rest the whole merits of their case upon the subject of religion. The race-feeling of the northern Irish against the English was so strong that it even extended to and was directed against the Roman Catholics of the Pale because they were of English descent. Whilst Ambrose Bedell, son

---

[1] For evidence as to the prosperous condition of Ireland before 1641 see Leland, iii. 41; Clarendon's *Irish Rebellion*, pp. 6-9; O'Conor's *Historical Address*, pt. ii. p. 255; Carte's *Ormond*, i. 87, folio ed.; Sir George Radcliffe's *Essay towards a Life of Lord Strafford*. Richard Belling, in his *History of the Irish Confederation*, gives very strong testimony to the same effect.

[2] Carte's *Ormond*, i. 178.

of the well-known Bishop Bedell, was prisoner among the rebels, he often heard the Ulster Irish threatening those of the Pale and using such expressions to them as these, "You churls with the great breeches, do you think that, if we were rid of the other English, we would spare you? No! for we would cut all your throats, for you are of one race with them, though we make use of you for the present."[1]

When the rebellion broke out, more than two-thirds of the landed property of Ireland was in the hands of the Roman Catholics, who were Celts either by blood or by traditions.[2] This one fact, of which there is not the slightest doubt, reveals to us the striking difference between the way the Normans acted in England and that in which the English acted in Ireland; and brings out the startling contrast between the conduct of the Saxon after the conquest and that of the Irish native after the English invasion. In England, after the battle of Hastings, there was not a single estate, certainly not one that was desirable in a Norman's eye, which was not transferred to one of the invaders. Yet the despoiled Saxon, after a few generations, forgot his wrongs and coalesced with his conqueror to form with him a national unity. In Ireland, notwithstanding some cases of encroachment, the Celt over the greater portion of the country was left in possession of his land. But the Irish native has ever sullenly refused to unite loyally with the Englishman and to share his labours and progress. To him time has brought no amnesty of complaints, no limitation of offences, and no healing on its wings. The reason of the difference in the conduct of the Saxon and the Celtic communities is not far to seek. Long before the Norman conquest the steady pressure of force had consolidated

[1] Deposition of Ambrose Bedell, Hickson's *Ireland in the Seventeenth Century*, i. 218.
[2] Sir William Petty's *Political Anatomy of Ireland*. Colonel Laurence says the Roman Catholics before the rebellion owned ten acres to one possessed by the English.—*The Interest of Ireland*, pt. ii. c. 2.

the Saxon principalities into a kingdom, and the idea of a single sovereign and central power had taken a firm hold on the English mind. But nothing like this had happened in Ireland, where a crowd of chiefs exercised perpetual wars against one another. The tribal or clannish spirit, which is wholly antagonistic to the conception of a State or to union under a strong central authority, survived in the Irish Celt.[1] It was this spirit which disabled him in the past from raising himself to the idea of a united nation: it is the same spirit which at the present time disqualifies him from conceiving that of an Empire. So deeply is this notion of a limited separate interest apart from the general interests of the common weal, engrained in the Irish mind, that it has been introduced into our parliamentary system by the representatives of Celtic Ireland. These representatives, unable to grasp the conception of serving for the whole realm, have cast aside the sacred duty of voting freely and independently according to their conscience. They have bound themselves by a covenant to sit, act, and vote, not as the interests of the Empire demand, but according as a majority of themselves shall dictate.[2]

The failure of Great Britain to conciliate the Irish Celt is but a temporary one. For it is not for want of the incorporating genius that she has not succeeded in this case. The British race has proved, and is daily proving, its capacity for absorbing and assimilating alien and foreign nationalities. The Scotch, Welsh, and Cornish Celts are hardly distinguish-

---

[1] A keen observer remarked the disintegrating effects of the tribal system in Gaul. *In Gallia*, says Cæsar, *non solum in omnibus pagis partibusque, sed pene etiam in singulis domibus factiones sunt.*

[2] This covenant runs as follows: "I pledge myself that in the event of my election to Parliament I will sit, act, and vote with the Irish parliamentary party; and if at a meeting of the party, convened upon due notice specially to consider the question, it be determined by a resolution supported by a majority of the entire parliamentary party, that I have not fulfilled the above pledge, I hereby undertake forthwith to resign my seat."

able from the rest of our nation. Danes and Normans have for centuries sunk into the general body of the people. The French Huguenots and the Flemish artisans have long forgotten the land and the tongue of their fathers. The Hindoo, the Mussulman, the Sikh, and the Buddhist are pressing eagerly into the family of the imperial mother. Of the three hundred millions of British subjects, more than a third of the human race, three and a half millions only—Irish Celts—stand apart sullen and discontented. The Irish branch of the great Celtic family alone remains unreconciled. It is the only one among the Celtic communities which has given up its own tongue and adopted that of the invader, together with his manners, customs, arts, and literature, and has at the same time refused to consider itself a child of the same household with the stranger. Yet there is nothing in the Celtic nature which presents a perennial bar to complete incorporation. Not to speak of the cases of Scotland, of Wales, and of Cornwall, the Celts of Gaul borrowed the language and civilisation of Rome, and became in time as Roman as the Romans themselves.

The rebellion of 1641 lasted more than eleven years, for it was not until the 27th of September 1653 that the Parliament was enabled to declare it at an end. It would be impossible within a limited space to give even a sketch of the boundless confusion and universal misery of these disastrous years. Europe has never witnessed, even in the Thirty Years' war, such a scene of discord and anarchy as prevailed in this small island during this period. It is wearisome to read, it would be useless, if possible, to relate the innumerable complications, transformations, entrances and exits, which took place.[1] There were always five parties in the field, sometimes

---

[1] Thus Owen Roe O'Neill was (1) opposed to Munro and the Ormondists; (2) to the Confederates, while he supported the Nuncio and the papal party; (3) he joined the parliamentary party and relieved Londonderry, which Coote held for that party; Owen receiving £2000 in money, some ammunition, and 2000 cows; (4) he

six,—the Northern Irish, the Royalists under Ormond, the Confederates of Kilkenny, the parliamentary party, the Nuncio's party, and Munro's Presbyterians. Though we can but glance at the actors and events of the rebellion, we are only too well acquainted with its fatal results. The historian[1] informs us that "the desolation of the island was complete. One third of the people had perished or been driven into exile. Famine and plague had finished the work of the sword. The fields lay uncultivated; and the miserable remnants of the flying population were driven to live on carrion and human corpses. The wolves so increased in numbers, even around the city of Dublin itself, that the counties were taxed for their extermination, and rewards were paid of five pounds for the head of a full-grown wolf, and two pounds for that of a cub."[2]

When the English Government at the close of the rebellion had obtained possession of the country, and subdued the factions which had so long preyed on the vitals of Ireland, the parliamentary scheme for the settlement of Ireland was carried into effect. The plan had been drawn up in August 1652, before the complete pacification of the country, and is to be found among the Acts of that year.[3] This plan

finally agreed to unite with Ormond, and was on his march to join him when he died at Cloughouter, 6th November 1649. The career of Ebher MacMahon, Bishop of Clogher, was as variable as that of Owen O'Neill.

[1] Walpole.

[2] Ludlow says that at the end of the war "a proclamation was published forbidding the killing of lambs and calves for the year next ensuing, that the country might recover a stock again, which had been so exhausted by the wars that many of the natives who had committed all manner of waste upon the possessions of the English were driven to such extremities that they starved with hunger; and I have been informed by persons deserving credit that the same calamity fell upon them even in the first year of the rebellion through the depredations of the Irish; and that they roasted men and eat them to supply their necessities."—*Memoirs*, i. 338.

[3] "Settling of Ireland," c. 13, 1652. Scobell's *Acts and Ordinances*, p. 197.

will ever be regarded with different eyes by two classes of readers. One class, fixing its attention on the sufferings of individuals and the vicissitudes of families, will deplore the misfortunes of ancient and respectable houses, and exclaim against the scheme and its projectors. The other class will merge their compassion for individuals in their indignation at the misery of the great body of the people brought to destruction by the sins and wickedness of their natural leaders. The general scope of the settlement was to punish the Irish aristocracy and gentry who had misgoverned their country, arrested the growing prosperity of Ireland, and plunged the land into a scene of bloodshed and anarchy compared with which the French Revolution was a peaceful reform. The object of the settlement was to bring home and limit the punishment to the castle and mansion, while it held out security and protection to the cottage and the hovel. The settlement has been misrepresented, but it remains in black and white, and ought to be examined and consulted by all who wish to have clear and distinct ideas respecting it. The first thing which strikes a reader of it is its leniency.[1] It was *not* a plan for the transplantation of a whole community, but for the removal of the leaders of that community, who had neglected the laws upon which societies are based,

---

[1] Here are *all* the provisions of the Settlement with the exception of two, which relate to estates tail and individuals under articles of surrender :—

"1. 'All husbandmen, ploughmen, labourers, artificers and others of the inferior sort' are received into protection. They and all persons 'having no real estate nor personal estate to the value of ten pounds' [a sum equivalent to £50 now] are pardoned for any act or thing done during the rebellion.

"2. All who before the 10th of November 1642 contrived or promoted the rebellion, murders, and massacres, excepted from pardon.

"3. Jesuits and priests who had contrived or promoted the rebellion, or any of the murders and massacres, excepted.

"4. A hundred and six Anglo-Irish and Irish persons excepted by name.

who had turned their country into a hell upon earth for twelve long years, and who had caused the death of more than half a million of their fellow citizens. The follies and crimes of the Irish aristocracy and gentry were infinitely greater than those which the French aristocracy and gentry expiated a hundred and fifty years later by a universal confiscation and their own decimation. The Irish had established a government in opposition to that of England; they had convened a general assembly of their nation regularly formed into Lords and Commons; raised armies and appointed generals; erected courts of justice; drawn up a new oath of allegiance; despatched envoys to invite foreign powers, the Pope, Emperor, and King of France, to lend their assistance; and finally they had hawked the crown of Ireland about Europe, and offered it to any Catholic prince who would take it under his protection. Yet the punishment which overtook the Irish aristocracy was infinitely less severe than that which befell the nobility and gentry of France.

"5. Principals and accessories to the murder of private persons, not officers either in the English or Irish armies, excepted.

"6. Twenty-eight days, after publication of a future notice, allowed to persons in arms to submit, otherwise excepted.

"7. Persons who had borne high commands, as generals, colonels, governors of forts, marshals of provinces, etc., to be banished during pleasure of Parliament and to forfeit two-thirds of their estates; lands to the value of the remaining third to be assigned to their wives and children in such parts of Ireland as the Parliament should determine.

"8. Power to parliamentary commissioners or commander-in-chief to declare pardon for their lives to all other persons who had been in arms; such persons, however, to forfeit two-thirds of their estates, lands to the value of the remaining third to be assigned them in such parts of Ireland as the Parliament should determine.

"9. All Roman Catholic proprietors who had resided in Ireland from the commencement of the rebellion to the 1st of March 1650, and had not manifested their constant good affection to the Commonwealth, to forfeit one-third of their lands; lands to the value of the other two-thirds to be assigned them in such places as the Parliament should think fit. All others who had not manifested 'their good affection' to forfeit one-fifth."

Not a head of the whole Irish body fell upon the scaffold except for private murder,[1] and when the convulsion had been brought to a close, a decent competence in land was allowed its members for the support of themselves and their families.

After the rebellion the landed property which remained in the hands of the Roman Catholics amounted to about one hundred thousand Irish acres of *profitable* lands in the other parts of Ireland, and seven hundred thousand acres of the same kind in Connaught and Clare.[2] This proportion continued down through the interregnum till the restoration of Charles II in 1660.[3]

When in 1655, at the end of the rebellion, the English settlers obtained possession of the lands which were distributed to them under the Parliamentary Settlement, the desolation of the country was complete. Ireland was a wilderness, over which the storms of war, of pestilence, and of famine had raged without intermission for twelve years. But the adventurers and soldiers set to work with a will, aided by the peasants, who remained in their homes as tenants or servants to the new proprietors. Industry, as usual, was followed by its natural results, and Ireland soon began to put on a new face. Even Clarendon, the author of the absurd story that the English Parliament intended the extermination of the Irish, admits that the country flourished to an unexampled extent under this arrangement. Two pictures of the state of Ireland, one of its condition before

---

[1] Sir Phelim O'Neill was not only tried for treason, but for being accessory to six murders.—Hickson's *Ireland in the Seventeenth Century*, i. 157.

[2] *State of the Papist and Protestant properties in Ireland in* 1641, 1653, *and* 1662. In the Thorpe collection.

[3] Sir William Petty estimated the surface of Ireland in this way— 10,500,000 Irish acres = 16,800,000 English acres, of which 3,000,000 were bogs, unprofitable land, etc., leaving 7,500,000 = 12,000,000 English measurement of good land. Ireland actually contains 20,815,460 English acres; so that Petty underestimated the contents of the country by a little more than four millions of English acres.

the Parliamentary Settlement, and the other subsequent to it, will give us an idea of the misery to which the Irish aristocracy and the priesthood had reduced the island, and of the prosperity which sprang up with the order and industry introduced by the settlers. Colonel Richard Laurence, a parliamentary officer, and afterwards a member of the Council of Trade in the reign of Charles II, is the author of the first :—

"About the years 1652 and 1653 the plague and famine had swept away whole countries, that a man might travel twenty or thirty miles and not see a living creature, either man, beast, or bird, they being either all dead or had quit those desolate places, that our soldiers would tell stories of the place where they saw a smoke, it was so rare to see either smoke by day or fire or candle by night; and when we did meet with two or three poor cabins, none but very aged men with women and children, and those with the prophet might have complained, *We have become as a bottle in the smoke, our skin is as black as an oven because of the terrible famine.* I have seen those miserable creatures plucking stinking carrion out of a ditch black and rotten, and have been credibly informed they have digged corps out of the grave to eat. But the most tragical story I ever heard was from an officer commanding a party of horse hunting for tories in a dark night, [who] discovered a light which they supposed to be a fire, which the tories usually made in those waste countries to dress their provisions and warm themselves; but drawing near they found it a ruined cabin, and besetting it round some did alight and peep in at the window, where they saw a great fire of wood and a company of miserable old women and children sitting round it, and betwixt them and the fire a dead corpse lay broiling, which as the fire roasted they cut off collops and eat."[1]

Clarendon presents us with the subsequent picture :—

"And which is more wonderful, all this [the Parliamentary Settlement] was done and settled within little more than two years, to that degree of perfection that there were many buildings raised for beauty as well as use, orderly and regular plantations of trees, and raising fences and enclosures throughout the kingdom, purchases made by one from the other at very valuable

---

[1] *The Interest of Ireland in its Trade and Wealth*, ii. 86.

rates, and jointures made upon marriages, and all other conveyances and settlements executed as in a kingdom at peace within itself, and where no doubt could be made of the validity of titles."[1]

At the commencement of the reign of Charles II in 1660 the three provinces of Ulster, Leinster, and Munster were, with the exception of the remnant which had been left to the Roman Catholics who had shown a constant good affection to the commonwealth, in the possession of the adventurers and soldiers. The contents of these provinces amounted to sixteen millions of English acres. The restoration upset completely the settlement which had been effected by the Parliament. Whatever legal title the adventurers might have to their lands, inasmuch as their claims rested on Acts[2] of Parliament which had been assented to by Charles I before the war, the soldiers knew that the courts of justice would not recognise their rights which were based on parliamentary ordinances only. But the adventurers and soldiers were well aware that their cause was one and the same. They therefore united, and after careful consideration they politicly determined to submit their interests to the king. Charles issued his declaration for the settlement of Ireland and for the satisfaction of the several interests on the 30th of November 1660. The Act of Settlement professed to be founded on this declaration, and to have for its object the execution and carrying out of the same. For this purpose, by one sweeping clause, it vested in the king three-fourths of the whole land of Ireland. There can be little doubt that Charles was unfavourably disposed to the Cromwellian occupants, the large majority of whom were nonconformists, and who were regarded by him as Republicans. But the king was prudent enough to see that he could not act against

---

[1] Works of Lord Clarendon, 2 vol. edition, ii. 1028.
[2] 17 Chas. I, cc. 34, 35, 36, 37.

the wishes of the English Parliament, which would not consent to hand back Ireland to the authors of its late evils. The Act of Settlement did not give satisfaction, and its complement, the Act of Explanation, was passed in 1665. This latter Act was essentially a compromise between the several contending parties, and ought to have been regarded as final by them all.[1] For to render such an arrangement possible, the adventurers and soldiers, at the request of the forfeited Roman Catholic proprietors, voluntarily gave up a third of their lands. The Act was understood by the Protestant owners to be a final settlement. But the Irish claimants never intended to abide by a compromise which they themselves had proposed. They accepted what the Act gave them, and waited for an opportunity of recovering all. An occasion arrived which to their blind greed appeared to be a propitious one. They grasped at all, and in the attempt they effected the ruin of their country and of themselves.

The result of these two Acts was, as Sir William Petty informs us, that the Roman Catholics obtained possession of about a third of the *profitable* land of Ireland, viz. 2,280,000 Irish acres or 3,648,000 English acres. If we remember that coarse land was excluded from this computation, and that Petty underestimated the superficial contents of Ireland by four millions of English acres, the Roman Catholic proprietors must have had in their hands at the accession of James II between five and six millions of English acres.

The prosperity which set in with the parliamentary or

[1] "The Roman Catholics at last, to end all disputes, proposed that if for the satisfaction of their interests the adventurers and soldiers would part with one-third of the lands respectively enjoyed by them on 7th May 1659 in consideration of their adventures and service, they were ready to agree to it. This proposal was in fine accepted. . . . Thus was the settlement of Ireland at last effected by the common consent of the agents of all the several interests concerned."—Carte's *Ormond*, ii. 303. See also the report of the English Attorney-General, Sir Heneage Finch, dated 1st February 1671.—Carte, Append.

Cromwellian Settlement continued during the whole reign of Charles II. We have several glowing accounts of the condition of Ireland during this reign, and at the accession of James, drawn by contemporaries and eye-witnesses. But three only shall be referred to here, those of Chief-Justice Keating, Archbishop King, and a gentleman who took refuge in England from the troubles of 1688. That of the Chief-Justice I shall quote hereafter, when describing the subsequent desolation. The agreement between all these descriptions, though by different hands, is very striking.

Archbishop King tells us that at King James's "coming to the crown, Ireland was in a most flourishing condition. Lands were everywhere improved, and rents advanced to near double what they had been a few years before. The kingdom abounded with money; trade flourished, even to the envy of our neighbours; cities, especially Dublin, increased exceedingly; gentlemen's seats were built or building everywhere; and parks, enclosures, and other ornaments were carefully promoted, insomuch that many places of the kingdom equalled the improvements of England. . . . And the king's revenue increased proportionably to the kingdom's advance in wealth, and was every day growing. It amounted to more than three hundred thousand pounds per annum—a sum sufficient to defray all the expenses of the crown, and to return yearly a considerable sum into England, to which this nation had formerly been a constant expense."

The account[1] given by the refugee is equally positive. "By the favour of heaven upon the extraordinary fertility of the land, Ireland was under very auspicious circumstances. The Church flourished, trade increased, the cities and towns were every year enlarged with new additions, the country enriched and beautified with houses and plantations; the farms were loaden with stock, and ready and quick markets

[1] *Apology for the Protestants of Ireland*, 1689.

there were to vent them. The laws had a free and uninterrupted course, and a standing army was so far from being a terror that they were the comfort and security of the people. In a word, peace, wealth, and plenty were become universal and epidemical, and all things conspired to a generous emulation with our mother and neighbour, England."

Such was the condition of Ireland at the accession of James. That of the Roman Catholic subject was equally favourable. The position of the Irish Roman Catholic was very different from and far superior to that of his English co-religionist. The penal enactments on the Irish Statute Book were fewer and less severe than those in England. In England every priest who received a convert into the bosom of the Church of Rome was liable to be hanged. In Ireland he incurred no such danger. A doubtful but favourable construction was placed on the Irish Act of Supremacy, and enabled Roman Catholics to fill public offices. "In England," says Macaulay, "no man could hold office, or even earn his livelihood as a barrister or a schoolmaster, without previously taking the oath of supremacy; but in Ireland a public functionary was not held to be under the necessity of taking that oath unless it were formally tendered to him. It therefore did not exclude from employment any person whom the Government wished to promote. The sacramental test and the declaration against transubstantiation were unknown; nor was either House of Parliament closed against any religious sect." In truth the state of the Irish Roman Catholics was much better than that described by Macaulay, and deserves a short consideration. For it will be seen how, when a legal toleration was within their reach, they refused to hold out their hands for it, and disqualified themselves from attaining it by declining to give a proof of their fidelity and allegiance to the government.

Shortly after the restoration of Charles II a petition was

presented to the English House of Peers in favour of the Roman Catholics, and a motion was made in the House for a relaxation of the penal laws. It was known that the king was in favour of the proposal, and the Lords were unanimous, "there not appearing one lord in the house who seemed to be unwilling that those laws should be repealed."[1] A committee was appointed to examine and report on the penal statutes. As soon as the committee was appointed, the Catholic peers and their friends were diligent in their attendance for some days, but on a sudden the committee was discontinued and was never subsequently revived. The truth was that the Roman Catholics had quarrelled amongst themselves. Dissensions had broken out between their laity, their secular and their regular clergy. Some meetings of a general committee, consisting of their principal lords, the superiors of orders, and the secular priests, were held at Arundel House. Difficulties were started at these meetings respecting the form of an oath or subscription which, it was intended, should be taken by Roman Catholics; and also respecting a proposition, that none but secular priests under bishops should be allowed in England, and that all regulars should be forbidden the kingdom. There had long been grave disputes and differences among the English Roman Catholics respecting their internal government and the oath of allegiance; these were revived on this occasion and the general committee was dissolved to meet no more.[2]

The prospect of relief afforded by the action of the English House of Lords and the known partiality of Charles encouraged the Irish Roman Catholic clergy and laity in 1661

---

[1] Clarendon's *Life*; Rev. Joseph Berington's *Memoirs of Panzani*, p. 309.

[2] Clarendon's *Life*; Berington, p. 310. A full account of the dissensions which had prevailed for eighty years among the English Roman Catholics is to be found in Berington's *Panzani*, and also in Sir John Throckmorton's *Letters to the Catholic Clergy of England*.

to petition the king for a mitigation of the laws which affected them. The conduct of this clergy[1] during the rebellion of 1641 had been so mad, reckless, and disloyal that it was felt to be useless to present a petition without a renunciation of the principles on which they had acted during that period.[2] They were advised to incorporate in their petition a declaration of their sentiments respecting the obedience and allegiance which was due from them to the Civil Power. This advice was given in order to get rid of the grand objection to their claims, namely, that the toleration of the Roman Catholic

---

[1] The Duke of Ormond, who knew them well, describes the Roman Catholic clergy of these times as "the worst spiritual guides that ever led a poor people to destruction."—Ormond to Orrery. The letter is given in French's *Unkinde Desertor*, 1676.

[2] It would be impossible to overstate the crimes and follies of the Irish Roman Catholic bishops and clergy during the rebellion. The following are some and only some of them :—

1. The Synod of Armagh, within six months after the breaking out of the insurrection, pronounced it to be lawful and pious.

2. On the 10th of May 1642, that is within eight months of the same period, a general synod declared it to be just and lawful.

3. At the last synod it was resolved to send envoys to the Pope, Emperor, and King of France to solicit assistance.

4. The bishops and clergy opposed the peace of 1646 with the king, excommunicated their own commissioners who negotiated it, and forbade the celebration of divine service in all towns and cities adhering to it.

5. They deposed the Supreme Council and assumed the government themselves.

6. They opposed the cessation of arms with Inchiquin on the ground that he was a heretic, and excommunicated its adherents.

7. They excommunicated the king's lord-lieutenant and drove him from the country.

8. They applied to the Pope to become protector of Ireland ; on the Pope's refusal they made a treaty with the Duke of Lorraine, vesting royal authority in him with the title of Protector Royal of Ireland.

9. They veered round from their former protestations of loyalty and favoured the progress of the parliamentary arms. They refused to excommunicate those who joined Cromwell or helped him with contributions or supplies. Hence the open markets, and the provisions sold freely in Cromwell's camp ; a state of things which Carlyle attributes to Cromwell's justice and ready money.

religion was inconsistent with the safety of a Protestant State. Accordingly Sir Richard Belling,[1] formerly secretary to the Kilkenny Confederation, drew up what was afterwards known as the Loyal Remonstrance of the Roman Catholic Clergy of Ireland. For the purpose of drawing up this document Belling made use of three negative propositions contained in a declaration signed by a great number of English Roman Catholics and presented to the Parliament in 1647.[2]

[1] This was the gentleman who, when envoy of the confederation, induced the Pope to send Rinuccini to Ireland.

[2] "The Roman Catholics of this nation, taking into consideration the twelve proposals of his Excellency Sir Thomas Fairfax [that the penal statutes should be repealed, and that the Roman Catholics should enjoy liberty of conscience by grant from the Parliament] lately published this present year 1647, and how prejudicial and destructive it might be to them at this time tacitly to permit an opinion (by some conceived) of an inconsistency in their religion with the civil government of this kingdom by reason of some doctrines and positions scandalously laid upon them, which might thereby draw on persons that cannot conform themselves to the religion here established an incapacity to receive and be partakers of a general benefit intended for the ease of tender consciences, have thought it convenient to endeavour the just vindication of their integrities therein. And to remove the scandal out of all the minds and opinions of moderate and charitable persons, do declare the negative to these propositions following :—

"I

"That the Pope or Church hath power to absolve any person or persons whatsoever from his or their obedience to the Civil Government established in this nation.

"II

"That it is lawful by the Pope's or Church's command or dispensation to kill, destroy, or otherwise injure any person or persons whatsoever, because he or they are accused or condemned, censured or excommunicated for error, schism, or heresy.

"III

"That it is lawful in itself or by the Pope's dispensation to break either word or oath with any person abovesaid, under pretence of their being heretics."—Walsh, *History of the Remonstrance*, pp. 522, 523. This declaration was condemned the following year by Innocent X, and its subscribers censured by a particular decree.—Throckmorton, *1st Letter*, p. 145.

Changing the words as required by the new circumstances of the case, Belling followed closely the expressions and intentions of the English petition.

The Irish Remonstrance acknowledged the king to be the supreme lord and rightful sovereign of Ireland; that the clergy were bound to obey him in all civil and temporal affairs, and to pay him loyalty and obedience notwithstanding any sentence or declaration of the Pope; it disclaimed all foreign power, papal or princely, spiritual or temporal, that should pretend to free them from this obligation; and declared that all princes of what religion soever were independent under God; and that it was impious and against the Word of God to maintain that any private subject might kill the prince though of a different religion.

A copy of this Remonstrance was sent to London and there signed by twenty-three Roman Catholic ecclesiastics and ninety-seven of the Irish nobility and gentry who were in that city. It was then presented to the king, and was received most graciously by him.

As the prospect was held out to the Roman Catholics of Ireland of obtaining relief from the penal laws, it became desirable to know whether the Remonstrance represented the real opinions of their clergy on the question of allegiance and obedience to the Civil Power. If it did, there could be no objection to an acknowledgment by that body of their loyalty to the established government. If, on the other hand, it did not, all further discussion was at an end, and the State could only come to the conclusion that both the Roman Catholic clergy and the laity, over whom they exercised a dominant influence, were unfit to be admitted into the constitution. To prevent all excuses and subterfuges, and to give an opportunity for a free and fair discussion of the subject of civil obedience, the Duke of Ormond allowed a national Synod of the Roman Catholic clergy to be convened at Dublin. The Synod met on the 11th of June 1666, and continued its sittings till the 25th of the same month. But it soon appeared that the Irish clergy still clung to a dogma which has since been given up by the Roman Catholic world; namely, that the Pope has the power of deposing kings and of dispensing with the allegiance due to them from their subjects. The Synod declined to sign the Loyal Remonstrance, and drew up on the 16th of June what they called "a remonstrance and protestation of their loyalty." This latter document contained no denial of the Pope's deposing power, and when read by the light of that doctrine was evasive and offered no guarantee of their loyalty and obedience to the Civil Power.

No sooner had it become known at Rome that it was proposed by the Roman Catholic clergy of Ireland to present a declaration of their loyalty to the Civil Power than the thunders of the Vatican were heard. The Nuncio at Brussels, De Vecchiis, who then exercised a superintendence over Irish religious affairs, condemned in July 1662 the Remonstrance on the ground that it denied the Pope's deposing power.[1] In the same month Cardinal Barberini, in a letter addressed to the noblemen and gentry of Ireland,[2] declared that the Remonstrance was a violation of the Catholic faith. And shortly before the meeting of the Synod in 1666, Rospigliosi, then Nuncio at Brussels and afterwards Cardinal, wrote to the Irish bishops and clergy that subscription to the Remonstrance would be grievous and hurtful to the Catholic religion.[3] In thus condemning a declaration of their loyalty by the Roman Catholics of Ireland, the Roman court and its ministers continued a policy on which they had long acted. In 1646 their own Nuncio, Rinuccini, on an occasion when he wanted to gain the Irish nobility and gentry to his designs,

---

[1] Throckmorton's *Letters to the Catholic Clergy*, etc., p. 154.
[2] *Ad præstantes viros Hiberniæ.*—Walsh, p. 17.
[3] Walsh, p. 633.

made a speech in which he boasted of his fidelity to the Royal cause. He was at once reprimanded from Rome for having used such expressions. Cardinal Pamphili, the Pope's Secretary of State, wrote to him in these words: "The Holy See never can by any positive act approve of the civil allegiance of Catholic subjects to a heretical prince. From this maxim of the Holy See have arisen many difficulties and disputes in England about oaths of allegiance. And His Holiness's displeasure is the greater because you have left the original of your speech in the hands of the Catholic confederates, which, if published, will furnish heretics with arguments against the Pope's power over heretical princes, seeing that his minister exhorts the Catholics of Ireland to allegiance to a heretical king."[1]

Again in December of the same year Pamphili informed Rinuccini "That it had been the constant and uninterrupted practice of the Holy See never to allow its ministers to make or to consent to any public edict of Catholic subjects for the defence of the crown and person of a heretical prince; that his conduct furnished pretences to the enemies of the Holy See to reflect upon her as deviating from the maxims of sound policy to which she had ever yet adhered; and that the Pope desired that he would not by any public act show that he knew or consented to any declaration of allegiance which Irish Catholics might for political reasons be compelled or be willing to make to the king."[2]

It is now admitted by all Roman Catholics that both the oath of allegiance drawn up by James I in England in 1605,

---

[1] Carte's *Ormond*, i. 578; O'Conor's *Historical Address*, pt. ii. p. 415, and the authorities there quoted. On receipt of this letter, Rinuccini, pretending that he had lost his own copy of the speech, applied to Lord Mountgarret, President of the Supreme Council, for the original, and returned in its stead a mutilated copy from which the offensive passage was omitted.—Carte's *Ormond*; O'Conor's *Historical Address*.

[2] O'Conor's *Historical Address* and Hutton's *Rinuccini*, p. 580.

and the Irish Remonstrance of 1662, are perfectly free from any objection, and contain nothing inconsistent with their faith or with their duty to the head of their church.[1] James knew that some Roman Catholics whose civil principles were sound and loyal seriously objected to the oath of supremacy. He therefore drew up a political test in the oath of allegiance to which it was thought all Catholics would cheerfully subscribe.[2] When this oath was first proposed it " was eagerly and generally taken by many of the secular clergy, of the Benedictines, and of the lay Catholics,"[3] and also by the Arch-

---

[1] "The instrument [the Irish Remonstrance] is now acknowledged by Catholics to be perfectly free from objection."—Throckmorton's *Letters to the Catholic Clergy*, p. 155.

"James II, when Duke of York, took the oath of allegiance, and intimated his intention of enforcing it when king."—Butler's *Memoirs of the English Catholics*, ii. 220.

"The apostolic delegate, Blackwell, in the reign of James I, took the oath himself and advised the English Catholics to take it."—*Ib.* p. 211.

"Why was this oath condemned? I defy any Catholic to find anything in it repugnant to his religion."—Rev. Chas. O'Conor's *Historical Address*, pt. ii. p. 160.

"A slight attention to the nature of the condemned oath would have convinced them [the Catholic laity] that nothing by it was demanded of them which as subjects they ought to refuse, and that nothing was renounced in it which affected their religion."—Throckmorton, *2d Letter*, p. 91.

Butler says it was a lamentable error to refuse the oath.—*Memoirs of the English Catholics*, ii. 203.

"The oath accordingly when tendered was taken by many Catholics, laity and clergy, and a ray of returning happiness gleamed around them. But a cloud soon gathered on the seven hills; for it could not be that a test, the main object of which was an explicit rejection of the deposing power, should not raise vapours there."—Rev. Joseph Berington's *Panzani*, p. 75.

Father Walsh advised all Roman Catholics to take the oath of allegiance and to sign the Remonstrance. "May you . . . offer that you will at the choice of the Parliament either take the oath of allegiance . . . or sign the loyal formulary."—*Address to the Catholics*, etc.

[2] 3 Jas. I, c. 4, § 15. James's oath is generally known as that of allegiance, the oath of Elizabeth as that of supremacy.

[3] *Throckmorton*, p. 134.

priest Blackwell,[1] the apostolic delegate in England, who advised his flock to take it. There was at last, after so many years, a prospect of a *modus vivendi* being established between the English Roman Catholics and the Government; a reconciliation between them and the State under the protection of which they lived. But the bright scene was soon clouded. Paul V in a brief of the 23d of October 1606 condemned the oath as containing "many things adverse to faith and salvation." The authenticity of this brief was generally doubted, and the Roman Catholics continued to manifest their allegiance. On this a second brief followed in 1607, which established the validity of the former and enforced submission. In 1608 a third brief was issued repeating the condemnation of the oath, and ordering all priests who had taken it, and did not retract within a limited time, to be deprived of their faculties.[2] Finally in 1626 a fourth condemnation was published by Urban VIII.[3] The same unhappy policy was again adopted in 1662, and the Irish Remonstrance was also condemned.

Protestants are too apt in their criticisms to confound the essential tenets of the Roman Catholic faith with the behaviour and policy of the governors and directors of the Romish Church, and Roman Catholics naturally resent judgments which mix up divine things with the consequences of human frailty. But the political action of individuals, whether Popes or Cardinals, is open to the world, and may be praised

---

[1] The last of the Marian bishops, Watson, died in 1584. Contrary to the wish of the English Catholics, who desired the appointment of bishops, a new office and title were created. Blackwell was made archpriest and superior over the clergy of England and Scotland in 1598. Blackwell was deposed in 1608 for taking the oath of allegiance and recommending the Catholics of England to take it. See Throckmorton's *Letters* and Berington's *Memoirs of Panzani*.

[2] *Throckmorton*, pp. 135, 136.

[3] This was the Pope who, as Cardinal Newman informs us, declared that Rome bewailed with "tears of blood" the conduct of the Papacy towards England. *Video meliora proboque, deteriora sequor.*

or censured by all, either Catholics or Protestants. It is the unquestionable duty of every subject, and of every class of subjects, when called upon by the Supreme Power in the State, to give such assurance of his or their allegiance as that power may require, either by an oath or solemn declaration, provided there is nothing in the oath or declaration which is opposed to his or their faith and conscience. There was nothing contrary to Catholic faith or conscience in the oath of allegiance or in the Irish Remonstrance. Yet the Roman Catholics of England were forbidden to take the oath of allegiance; those of Ireland were prohibited from signing the Remonstrance. The authors of the briefs against the English oath and of the prohibitions against signing the Irish Remonstrance forbade the reception of the Roman Catholics of England and Ireland into our constitution, and shut the gates of admission in the face of millions of faithful and obedient believers who looked to them for guidance. These rulers and councillors, to maintain an ambitious claim which had no better foundation than the arrogance of former pontiffs and the "weak concessions of mortals," prevented a reconciliation of the members of their church with the governments under which they lived as subjects. Unwilling to give up an old and rusty weapon which had been opposed with success in every kingdom of Europe, and which they have since abandoned, the vicars of Him, whose *kingdom is not of this world*, left the Roman Catholics of these countries exposed to laws necessarily severe.[1] For the subject who refuses to give guarantees of his loyalty is justly suspect as

[1] "And Paul himself could sit undisturbed in the Vatican, hearing that men were imprisoned and that blood was poured out in support of a claim which had no better foundation, surely he knew, than the ambition of his predecessors and the weak concessions of mortals; he could sit and view the scene, and not in pity at least wish to redress their sufferings by releasing them from the injunctions of his decree."—Rev. Joseph Berington's *Panzani*, p. 86.

an enemy, and justly condemned to exclusion from the full rights of citizenship.

Notwithstanding the refusal of the Irish bishops and clergy to give a pledge of their loyalty and obedience to the State in all civil matters, the Roman Catholics of Ireland enjoyed from 1660 to the accession of James II a toleration which, when compared with the contemporaneous condition of the Protestant subjects under the Catholic Governments of Europe, was a state of perfect freedom. Archbishop King tells us that, when James came to the throne, there was "a free liberty of conscience by connivance though not by law." But as the evidence of this prelate is sometimes called in question, Roman Catholic testimony will be adduced. Father Walsh, writing in 1672, informs us that Charles II effectually countermanded "the winds and tempests of persecution throughout Ireland."[1] In his speech to the Synod in June 1666 the same ecclesiastic reminded the assembled fathers, who must have been acquainted with the facts, "of the ceasing of persecution, release of prisoners, general connivance at the exercise of their religion through all provinces and parts of Ireland, even within the walls of corporate towns and garrisons."[2] In the same month eighteen Catholic priests presented a petition or letter of expostulation to the Synod, advising the signature of the Remonstrance, in which these words occur: "Is it not further as manifestly apparent how graciously that instrument [the Remonstrance] after the signature of it was received by His Majesty? How immediately the persecution in this kingdom ceased by His Majesty's express commands. Nay, how ever since both people and clergy of our communion have enjoyed the great tranquillity

---

[1] Father Walsh informs us that at this time the number of secular priests was more than a thousand, and of the regulars eight hundred. Cardinal Moran, in his *Life of Archbishop Plunket*, estimates the seculars at a thousand and the regulars at six hundred.

[2] *History of the Remonstrance*, p. 654.

and freedom in point of exercising our religion and functions which we have so gladly seen and which we so thankfully acknowledge to be still continued to us, yea, in a higher measure enjoyed by us at this present than we could almost have not long since either believed or hoped we should live to see."[1] In 1670 the Lord Lieutenant received special instructions to favour and protect the remonstrant, that is the loyal, priests.[2] Archbishop Plunket writes in the same year to the Cardinal Protector at Rome: "The Viceroy of this kingdom shows himself favourable to the Catholics, not only in consequence of his natural mildness of disposition, but still more on account of his being acquainted with the benign intentions of His Majesty in reference to his Catholic subjects."[3] In another letter of the same year, addressed to the new pontiff, Clement X, the same prelate says : "We experience in this kingdom, Holy Father, the benign influence of the King of England in favour of the Catholics, so that all enjoy great liberty and ease. Ecclesiastics may be publicly known, and are permitted to exercise their functions without any impediment."[4] When the Duke of Ormond resumed the viceroyalty in 1677, Dr. Plunket "often speaks of his government as peaceful and mild."[5] Such was the general tenor of the conduct of the Government towards the Irish Roman Catholics, though it was sometimes disturbed for short intervals on occasions of national excitement, such, for example, as that which was consequent on the so-called Popish plot.

But the best test of the toleration granted to the Roman Catholics may be derived from their own conduct. Did they show by the humility of their proceedings that they considered themselves as oppressed and as excluded from freedom of action? Did their bishops and clergy refrain from the

---

[1] *History of the Remonstrance*, p. 698.
[2] *Life of Archbishop Plunket*, by Archbishop (now Cardinal) Moran, p. 48.   [3] *Ib.* p. 51.   [4] *Ib.* p. 52.   [5] *Ib.* p. 55.

open exercise of their functions, and was their carriage that of those who felt themselves to be persecuted? At or about this time it was death, or what was worse than death, the galleys, for a Protestant divine to celebrate the offices of his religion in the Catholic countries of Europe.[1] The conduct of the Roman Catholic ecclesiastics in Ireland presents a lively contrast to the state of things on the Continent. Within three months after his arrival from Rome in 1670 Archbishop Plunket "solemnised two synods of his clergy, and moreover convened and presided at a general synod of the Irish bishops, which was held in Dublin; and before the month of September in the same year we find him summoning a provincial council of Ulster, and enacting many salutary decrees for the correction of abuses and the advancement of ecclesiastical discipline in that province."[2] In 1678 the same prelate convoked another provincial synod at Ardpatrick, where decrees were made and enactments passed.[3] In 1670 Peter Talbot, titular Archbishop of Dublin, appeared before the Privy Council in his episcopal habits, a thing of which there had been no precedent since the Reformation. On another occasion the same archbishop applied to the Lord Lieutenant for the loan of some of the State hangings, silver candlesticks, plate, and other utensils, for the purpose of making use of them at the celebration of high mass. The request was complied with.[4] But this is not all: we are informed by Archbishop Plunket, in a letter to the Nuncio in the year 1673, that the same Peter Talbot, "during the past four years, waged an open war against the Duke of Ormond, who

---

[1] This subject is more fully treated in the following chapter.
[2] Moran's *Life of Archbishop Plunket*, p. 56.
[3] *Ib.* p. 58.
[4] The loan was accompanied with a complimentary message from the Lord Lieutenant's secretary, Sir Ellis Leighton, "that he hoped to have high mass at Christ Church at Christmas."—*Secret Consults*, etc. ; *State Tracts*, iii. 620 ; *Leland*, iii. 462.

is the most powerful subject of His Majesty in this kingdom."[1] Let us imagine, if we can, what would have been the fate of a Protestant ecclesiastic in Austria, Spain, France, or Savoy, who would at this time have opposed, not a powerful ex-viceroy, but even a parish officer. If we consider this, we shall be able to guess at the difference between the position of a Roman Catholic in Ireland and that of a Protestant in these Catholic kingdoms at this period. It is absurd and in the highest degree ungrateful for Irish Roman Catholic writers to speak of the conduct of the Government as oppressive at a time when the Protestant subjects of Catholic kingdoms were hunted like wolves or mad dogs, and persecuted, not as being dangerous to the safety of the State, but for holding religious opinions different from those professed by their rulers. If these partisans were acquainted with comparative history, they would thankfully acknowledge that their co-religionists enjoyed at this time in Ireland a toleration which was unknown to Catholic governments, and which was simply marvellous considering the spirit of the times and the disaffection of the subjects to whom it was extended—a disaffection which was so soon again to manifest itself, for the second time within forty years, at the expense of the ruin of the country and at the cost of a hundred thousand lives.

The condition and circumstances of the Roman Catholic laity at the accession of James II were as favourable as the position of the clergy. Archbishop King tells us that great numbers of them had acquired considerable estates "either by traffic or by the law, or by other arts and industries." And Colonel Laurence, writing in 1682, speaks strongly of their general prosperity at the time. "For," says he, "although a considerable number of them may be of desperate fortunes, being branches of those ruined families sequestered for former rebellions, to whom war is the best

[1] Moran's *Life of Archbishop Plunket*, p. 88.

trade and revenge desirable wages—if they gain nothing they cannot lose much. But this is not the case of the body of them. There are many of their nobility[1] and gentry enjoy plentiful estates with the favour and countenance of their prince, some of whom never quitted the interest of the Crown in the last twelve years' war, and now reap the profit of it. And multitudes of the commons are wealthy merchants in our cities and rich farmers in the country, who, although they be strict Papists, yet are friendly and good neighbours and just and honest dealers, who have as much reason to dread a war as the English themselves."[2]

[1] At the accession of James II the number of the Catholic peers was about forty.
[2] *Interest of Ireland in its Trade and Wealth,* ii. 89. When Colonel Laurence published this book he had been thirty-three years in Ireland.

SECTION II

THE PREPARATION FOR THE PARLIAMENT[1]

IT was in a country so circumstanced, rapidly advancing in prosperity,[2] and in which the Roman Catholic subject enjoyed a toleration which was absolute freedom when compared with the position of Protestants under the Catholic governments of Europe, that the king, Tyrconnel, and the Irish priesthood entered upon a conspiracy which was to end in the desolation of the island. The old attempts were to be renewed, and the old game of 1641, which had ended so disastrously, was to be played over again. But the conditions of the game were now altered. A king of Great Britain and his secret council[3] had joined the conspiracy. James had

---

[1] Portions of this and the following section appeared in a pamphlet which I published anonymously in Dublin, 1886.

[2] "This kingdom improves visibly, and it is improved beyond what could have been reasonably hoped for in the space of twenty years. Nor can anything but a civil war or some other of God's national judgments stop the career of prosperity it is in."—Ormond to the King, 1681; Carte, Append.

[3] It is from James's own statement that we have the most certain evidence of the existence of this secret council. "He [Sunderland] persuaded the king to appoint some of the most considerable Catholics to meet at certain times either at his office or at Mr. Chiffinch's to consult of matters relating to religion, and he pretending to be much inclined to and at the last professing himself a Catholic, was not only admitted, but soon had the chief direction of this secret juncto; it was a sort of committee from the Cabinet Council itself, whither by degrees he drew all business, and by consequence made himself umpire of the whole transactions relating to the Government."—Clarke's *Life of James II*, ii. 74.

found that his attack on the liberties and constitution of England was not as likely to succeed as he had once hoped. He was therefore resolved, as he informed some of his friends and followers who began to doubt the result of his schemes, to provide for himself and them "a sure sanctuary and retreat in Ireland if all those endeavours should be blasted in England which he had made for their security, and of whose success he had not yet reason to despair."[1] He determined therefore to exalt the power and influence of the Roman Catholic body in Ireland, and to destroy the Protestant or English interest in that country, in order that he and his party might have a refuge or fortified camp to which they could retreat, and from which they could either negotiate or defend themselves with the aid of France. To carry out this scheme James selected Tyrconnel as his instrument. Though Tyrconnel's appointment was opposed by every moderate English Roman Catholic about the king,[2] James insisted on his nomination. "There is work to be done in Ireland," said he, "which no Englishman will do."

Tyrconnel had long been the agent at the English Court of that Irish party which desired the repeal of the Acts of Settlement and the restoration of the Roman Catholics to the forfeited estates, a scheme which was dreaded by the English Catholics as dangerous and revolutionary. He was supported

---

[1] *Secret Consults*, etc.; *State Tracts*, iii. 616. "Jacques II dès le commencement de son regne, avoit fait visiter toutes les places militaires de cette ile par le lord Darmouth, grand maitre de l'artillerie d'Angleterre. Son rapport, qui est sous nos yeux, prouve le dessein forme d'arracher la preponderance aux Anglois et de former en Irlande un systeme de defense pour une hypothese qui s'est realisee; la necessite pour le Roi de se refugier parmi les Irlandois Catholiques." "Les desseins du Roi sur l'Irlande embrassoient l'espace de cinq années, le temps lui parassait necessaire pour fortifier le Royaume, et pour y preparer un asyle, independant de son successeur, aux Catholiques."— Mazure, *Révolution de* 1688, ii. 115, 287.

[2] Lord Bellasis said at the Council Board, "That fellow, Dick Talbot, is fool and madman enough to ruin ten kingdoms."

at the Court by the Queen and Father Petre, though opposed by the Privy Council and the House of Commons. This latter assembly had even petitioned Charles II in 1673 to dismiss him from all command, civil or military, and to forbid his appearance at Court. If but a part of what has been said of this man be true, he was a prodigy of wickedness. Some virtues at least enter into our conception of a political leader, but Tyrconnel appears to have been deficient in every quality required. There was neither conscience, veracity, nor prudence in the man. He was not even faithful to the family of the master to whom he owed everything.[1] If James had had the feelings of a man, he would have detested one who had attempted to blacken the good fame of his first wife. But Tyrconnel was the chosen leader of the Irish priesthood, and by their influence, backed by the king's knowledge of Tyrconnel's wish to destroy the Protestant interest in Ireland, James was induced to employ him, first as commander of the forces in that country, and afterwards as Lord Deputy. The recommendation of the Irish priesthood in favour of Tyrconnel is still extant.[2] It was found amongst the papers of Tyrrell, titular Bishop of Clogher, and secretary to Tyrconnel. An extract will show how highly Tyrconnel and his services were valued by the Irish clergy: "And since of all others the Earl of Tyrconnel did first espouse and chiefly maintain, these twenty-five years last past, the cause of your poor oppressed Roman Catholic clergy, and is now the only subject of your Majesty under whose fortune and popularity in this kingdom we dare cheerfully and with assurance own our loyalty and assert your Majesty's interest, do make it our humble suit to your Majesty, that you will be pleased to lodge your authority over us in his hands, to the terror of the

---

[1] Tyrconnel made overtures to France for casting off all connection with England, and, in the event of James's death, for placing the crown of Ireland on his own head.—Mazure, *Révolution de* 1688, ii. 287.

[2] King's *State of the Protestants*, Append.

factious and encouragement of your faithful subjects here. Since his dependence on your Majesty is so great, that we doubt not but that they will receive him with such acclamations as the long-captivated Israelites did their redeemer Mordecai. And since your Majesty in glory and power does equal the mighty Ahasuerus, and the virtues and beauty of your Queen is as true a parallel to his adored Hester, we humbly beseech she may be heard as our great patroness against that Haman[1] whose pride and ambition of being honoured as his master may have hitherto kept us in slavery."

We may well wonder that the Irish clergy should choose such a representative and leader. However this may be, it is certain that they and Tyrconnel, with the assent and concurrence of James, began a conspiracy against the liberties, property, and Church of the Protestants in Ireland. The aim of the conspiracy was threefold—Roman Catholic ascendency in this country, and the exclusion of Protestants from all civil and military employment; the complete separation of Ireland from England; and the restoration of the land to the Irish. The events subsequent to the commencement of the year 1685, and up to the landing of William, the conduct of James's Irish Government, and the legislation of the Irish Parliament, leave no doubt of the existence and aims of this conspiracy. The means intended to effect these aims were, first, to get possession of the whole civil, military, and judicial power in the nation; secondly, to master the representation; and thirdly, to call a Parliament which should give effect to their policy. If there are minds so constituted as to remain unconvinced by the logic of facts and conduct, at least they cannot refuse credence to written testimony. Among the letters of the same Tyrrell there was found one addressed to the king, in which the programme of the conspirators was clearly explained, and this programme was afterwards literally

[1] Ormond.

carried out. The letter is long, and in parts imperfect; but sufficient remains to indicate its scope and meaning.[1] The paragraph which refers to the means to be adopted for working out the ends of the conspiracy is here given. The writer, after recommending the king to promote Catholics to "the most eminent and profitable stations," and expressing a fear that the Protestants in his English army would be inclined to fight for the king, Parliament, and Protestant religion against the king as Papist, his Popish cabals, and popery, goes on to say: "To prevent which, as matters now stand, there is but one sure and safe expedient, that is, to purge without delay the rest of your Irish army, increase and make it wholly Catholic; raise and train a Catholic militia there; place Catholics at the helm of that kingdom; issue out *quo warrantos* against all the corporations in it; put all employs, civil as well as military, into Catholic hands. This done, call a Parliament of loyal"—here the document is illegible for a few lines. But the sketch is complete, and we shall soon see that the line of action recommended in this letter was at once put into operation. The letter was sent to James in August 1686, while Lord Clarendon was Lord Lieutenant, and Tyrconnel Commander-in-Chief in Ireland. The first step taken in prosecution of the conspiracy was

1. *The Disarming of the Protestants*

The Duke of Ormond, when Lord Lieutenant in the years 1662-69, had raised and armed a body of twenty thousand men as a militia, to protect the English settlers and to restrain the banditti which then infested the country. After the rebellion of Monmouth in England, under the pretence that this militia was well affected to his claims, an order came from England, while Lord Granard and Archbishop

[1] The letter is given in the Appendix to King's *State of the Protestants*.

Boyle were Lords Justices,[1] that its arms should be taken and deposited in magazines in each of the counties. The carrying out of the order was entrusted to Tyrconnel, and the militia was disarmed. But this was not sufficient. It was resolved to disarm *all* the Protestants, and to deprive them even of their private weapons, which were necessary for the defence of themselves or their houses. Accordingly "it was given out that if any arms were reserved under any pretence, such as that they were their own and not belonging to the public, it would be regarded as a proof of disaffection."[2] The terror inspired by this menace was so great that the Protestants delivered up the arms and weapons which they had bought with their own money and for their own protection. Though the settlers were obliged by the terms of their patents of plantation to keep arms in readiness for the king's service, and the country was in a very disturbed condition, they were deprived of all means of defence, and left "without any one weapon in their houses, and the Irish were all armed."[3] While this was being done, and the Protestants disarmed, the native Irish were, on the other hand, permitted by Tyrconnel to retain their weapons. We have in Lord Clarendon's letters an account of a warm debate which took place in the Privy Council on this matter. Many of its members—for the Protestants had not yet seceded from it—complained of the state of the country, and of the English settlers being left totally defenceless among a peasantry who were hostile to the Protestants and unwilling to aid them when attacked. The Lords Justices who were present declared that they had given orders to collect the arms of the militia only, but admitted that those of private persons also

---

[1] Lord Granard and the Chancellor, Archbishop Boyle, were Lords Justices between the recall of the Duke of Ormond in 1685 and the arrival of Lord Clarendon in January 1686.

[2] *Secret Consults*, etc.

[3] Clarendon to Lord Rochester, Clarendon's *Corr.* i. 217.

had been taken, under the pretence of disarming the militia. One of them, Lord Granard, added that this was done, he knew not "by what officiousness." We know by what and by whose officiousness it was done. This illegal measure was undertaken by Tyrconnel, and accomplished by him alone.

The natural consequences of this measure ensued. No sooner had the English settlers been disarmed than the banditti and rapparees issued from their haunts and commenced their outrages against the Protestants. Persons were set upon and dangerously wounded in the open day.[1] Houses were attacked, and the flocks and herds of the English driven away or destroyed. Crimes were so multiplied that Special Commissions had to be issued to clear the jails;[2] and, worst of all, the officers and soldiers of the army, which Tyrconnel was then engaged in filling up with Catholics, contributed to the outrages and the general disorganisation of the kingdom. They even interfered with the revenue officers in the discharge of their duties, and prevented the collection of the king's taxes.[3] The historian[4] tells us that these "new arms in new hands were made use of as might have been expected. The soldiers harassed the inhabitants, and lived upon them at free quarters. Tyrconnel, instead of punishing these offences, encouraged them." When soldiers were taken red-handed in the commission of crime, they were claimed by their officers from the civil power; and, in consequence of this conduct of the officers, magistrates refused to take examinations where any of the army were concerned.[5]

---

[1] Clarendon to Sunderland, Clarendon's *Corr.* i. 215, 230.
[2] Clarendon to Sunderland, *Corr.* ii. 106.
[3] Clarendon to Rochester, *Corr.* ii. 4.   [4] Dalrymple.
[5] "Some [the soldiers] are taken in committing felonies four or five miles from the town and carried before the next justice of the peace. . . . These things some of the officers are much dissatisfied at, thinking that men once in the king's pay must upon no pretence be taken hold of by the civil magistrate."—Clarendon to Sunderland, 18th December 1686. "The justices of the peace are very unwilling

Lord Clarendon complains of the excesses even of the officers, and mentions an extraordinary outrage committed by one of them, Lord Brittas, on the High Sheriff of a county. We give it in his own words, and the instance will show to what a state the country had been reduced. "The High Sheriff of the county sent an injunction out of Chancery to my Lord Brittas, to quit the possession of another man with whom his lordship has a suit. My lord beat the man most terribly who brought the injunction, and not being satisfied therewith, he took a file of his men with him, found out where the sheriff himself was, dragged him into the streets, and caused him to be beaten most cruelly, saying he would teach him how to carry himself towards the officers of the king's army." If such an outrage could be committed with impunity [1] against a high public officer, it is easy to imagine the condition of private persons.

These proceedings spread universal terror and alarm, and their effects soon showed themselves in the decline of the country. Trade and agriculture decayed rapidly; landlords hastened to sell their estates for whatever could be got; merchants closed their accounts, and withdrew themselves and their stocks to England; farmers threw up their leases; manufactories were shut up;[2] the revenue declined; an

to take examinations where any of the army are concerned, though I have signified to them that they need not fear doing their duty, especially where the lives of any of His Majesty's subjects are concerned." Clarendon to Sunderland, Clarendon's *Corr.*, ii. 137.

[1] This crime was not punished. Lord Brittas *apologised* for it to the Lord Lieutenant. This ruffian afterwards sat in the Dublin Parliament. Two equally shameful outrages are told of Lord Clancarty, another of Tyrconnel's officers.—*Secret Consults*, etc.

[2] "The other day, my Lord Chief Justice being with me and discoursing from his observations in his late circuit of the great decay of the inland manufactories and the damp that seemed to be upon the minds of the trading people and husbandmen, I said to him, etc. . . . I can myself give one instance of a man in the county of Cork who, about eighteen months since, had forty looms at work, and about six months since he put them all off; has given his landlord warning, for he was a great renter, that he will leave his lands. There is another

exodus, on a scale hitherto happily unknown in these islands, began. As early as June 1686 Lord Clarendon writes: "It is impossible to tell you the alterations that are grown in men within this month; but the last week—for I am very inquisitive to be informed of those particulars—one hundred and twenty people went in one ship from hence to Chester, and multitudes are preparing, from all parts of the kingdom, to be gone as fast as they can get in their debts and dispose of their stocks. Great sums of money are brought to town, and more is daily coming up to be sent away; and in regard the exchange is so high, for it is risen twenty shillings in £100 within these four days, and that no returns, even at these high rates, can be gotten into England, they are endeavouring to remit their money into France and Holland, to draw it from thence hereafter at leisure. In the meantime, there is no money in the country, and the native commodities yield nothing. The king's quit-rents and chimney-money come in very slowly. To distrain signifies nothing or very little, for the collector cannot sell the distress when he has taken it, that is, nobody will buy it."[1] And, again, in August of the same year: "Those traders who have got home their effects have withdrawn themselves and their stocks out of the kingdom, which is undeniable matter of fact. I can name several who paid the king many thousands a year to his duty who are absolutely gone, and left no factors to carry on their trade, by which means several thousands of natives, who were employed in spinning and carding of wool, are discharged and have no work. There are likewise multitudes of farmers and renters gone to England, who, though they were not men of estates, yet the improvements of the country and the

in the province of Munster, likewise, who keeps five hundred families at work. This man, sending to a tenant for £30 which he owed him, was presently accused by the said tenant of having spoken treasonable words."—Clarendon to his brother, 30th May 1686.

[1] Clarendon to Rochester, *Corr.* i. 464.

inland trade was chiefly carried on by them." In a word, the desolation which afterwards, within a few months, overtook the land was already settling down upon it; and Ireland, which only two years ago was, as Chief Justice Keating called it, "the most improved and most improving spot of ground in Europe," was fast becoming a desert. Most of the English inhabitants fled, and art, industry, and capital fled with them.

2. *The Exclusion of Protestants from the Army*

The army of Ireland, at the accession of James, consisted of about seven thousand men, " as loyal and as cordial to the king's service as any one could be; both officers and soldiers had been inured to it for many years. They looked on him as their master and father, entirely depending on him, and expecting nothing from anybody else. When Monmouth's and Argyle's rebellion called for their assistance to suppress them, no people in the world could show more cheerfulness or forwardness than they did. Most of the officers of this army had been so zealous to serve the king that they had by his permission and encouragement bought their employments; many of them had laid out their whole fortunes and contracted debts to purchase a command."[1] Tyrconnel, who was not able to put a regiment through its exercise,[2] came to Ireland as general of the forces in 1686, with blank commissions and with instructions to admit Roman Catholics into the army, which up to this time was exclusively Protestant. These instructions of the king implied no more than that all subjects indiscriminately should be admitted to his service. Tyrconnel himself admitted to Lord Clarendon that such was their meaning. But his declarations that no distinction should

---

[1] King.
[2] "Lord Tyrconnel himself, after all his infallible skill, cannot draw up a regiment, which is visible here."—Clarendon to Rochester, *Corr.* i. 436.

be made between Roman Catholic and Protestant differed greatly from the proceedings which at once commenced, for Tyrconnel was acquainted with the real wishes of the king.[1] Within a short time after his arrival, between two and three hundred officers were removed without any reason assigned. These gentlemen, who had bought their commissions, and many of whom had shed their blood for the crown, were dismissed without allowance or compensation. The letters of Lord Clarendon are full of the many hard cases of these officers, whom he knew to be good soldiers and loyal subjects. For some he pleaded with Tyrconnel in vain, and others he recommended to the king and his friends in England. The majority[2] went abroad, and many of them took service in Holland, thus swelling the number of William's friends and James's enemies. Of the persons who were appointed in their stead all were Roman Catholics, but this was the only qualification required. The majority consisted of such as were entirely ignorant of military duties, or were taken from the meanest of the people. Some had been grooms, some footmen, and some noted marauders. Archbishop King mentions the case of the famous rapparees, the Brannans, who were made officers,

---

[1] Dalrymple tells us that James afterwards complained that Tyrconnel exceeded his orders. The truth is, the statements of the king and of Tyrconnel are equally unworthy of credit. James says in his Memoirs that he was pleased with Tyrconnel's conduct; "to him [Tyrconnel], therefore, the king gave a power to regulate the troops, to place and displace whom he pleased, which he executed very much to the king's satisfaction and advantage." On the other hand, Tyrconnel informed Clarendon that the work was entirely the king's. Clarendon thus reports Tyrconnel: "Here are great alterations to be made and the poor people who are put out think it my doing, and G—— d—— me I have little or nothing to do in the matter; for I told the king that I knew not two of the captains, nor other inferior officers in the whole army. I know there are some hard cases which I am sorry for; but by G—— I know not how to help them. You must know, my lord, the king, who is a Roman Catholic, is resolved to employ his subjects of that religion."—*Corr.* i. 481.

[2] One of these dismissed officers was Gustavus Hamilton, afterwards Governor of Enniskillen, who did good service for King William.

and says that he had been informed that there were at least twenty tories officers in one regiment, and that there were very few regiments without some. Lord Clarendon complains of the excesses committed by these new officers, and points to great abuses committed by them with regard to the subsistence money of the army. "Scarce a colonel of the army," he writes, "knows anything of his regiment." D'Avaux, in one of his despatches, informs the French king that the colonels of the Irish army were generally men of good family, who had never seen service, but that the captains were butchers, tailors, and shoemakers.[1]

The change or remodelling of the army, as it was termed, was not limited to the officers. Tyrconnel, with equal brutality and disregard of common humanity, disbanded between five and six thousand common soldiers. The dismissal of the soldiers to beg through the country created even a greater sensation than that of the officers, "because their clothes having been taken from them when they were broke, they wandered, half naked, through every part of the kingdom."[2] In Dublin four hundred of the regiment of the guards were turned out in one day, three hundred of whom had no "visible fault."[3] The same thing was done at the same time throughout the country. The new officers received orders to enlist none but Roman Catholics.[4] "I will give you," says Lord Clarendon, "one instance only: Mr. Nicholas Darcy, who has the company late Captain Motloe's, called his com-

---

[1] "La plupart de ces regimens sont levez par dez gentils hommes qui n'ont jamais esté à l'armée. Ce sont des tailleurs, des bouchers, des cordonniers, qui ont formé les compagnies, et qui en sont les capitaines."

[2] Dalrymple. "This part he [Tyrconnel] acted in a most insulting barbarous manner, causing poor men that had no clothes on their backs but red coats to be stripped to their shirts and so turned off; and of all this he himself was an inhuman spectator."—*Secret Consults*, etc.

[3] Clarendon to Rochester, *Corr.* i. 476.

[4] "The turning out so many men in an instant, taking in none but natives in their room, and the very indiscreet conduct of some of the new officers in declaring they will entertain no English nor any Protestants, does frighten people."—Clarendon to Sunderland, *ib.* p. 485.

pany together, and asked them if they went to mass, to which forty of them said 'no,' whereupon he immediately dismissed them, and said he had kept as many above a week at his own house upon his own charge, who, the next morning, were all admitted." Of the class of recruits who replaced the veterans dismissed by Tyrconnel, let two contemporaries speak: "When any new men are listed, they are sent to the commissary to be sworn. The first thing they say is, that they will not take the oath of supremacy; he tells them he is not to tender it to them, therefore they need not fear; that they are only to take the oath of fidelity, which is the oath mentioned in my instructions, and taken by the Roman Catholic judges. That they swallow; and being asked whether they understood what they have sworn, the answer was, 'yes, they had been sworn to be true to the Pope and their religion;' and being told by some that they had been sworn to be true to the king, they replied, 'their priest had told them they must take no oath but to be true to the Pope.'"[1] The other witness is Mr. Stafford, a Roman Catholic who, through the interest of his son, lately appointed a Master in Chancery, had been made a Justice of the Peace. In a charge to the grand jury, at the quarter sessions held at Castlebar in October 1686, this gentleman naïvely remarked: "I shall not need to say much concerning rogues and vagabonds, the country being pretty well cleared of them, by reason His Majesty has entertained them all in his service, clothed them with red coats, and provided well for them."[2]

[1] Clarendon's *Corr.* i. 476.
[2] This charge is so amusing that the whole of it is here given. "Gentlemen, the spoiling of your garrans in their infancy, so that they are not afterwards fit to do His Majesty any service; of this beware, gentlemen. Next, your burning corn in the straw, contrary to an Act of Parliament. But perhaps this Lustrabane bread may palate your mouth very well; but you want the straw in winter to lie upon yourselves, for you generally lie upon straw, and for fodder for your cattle, so that you are forced to lift them up by the tail; of this also beware,

3. *The Remodelling of the Courts of Justice*

Lord Clarendon was dismissed at the end of 1686, and Tyrconnel arrived in Ireland, and was sworn in as Lord Deputy on the 11th February 1687. During Clarendon's administration Sir Charles Porter had been Lord Chancellor. He had been originally chosen because it was supposed that he held strong opinions in favour of absolute authority. But latterly he had shown himself restive at the proceedings of Tyrconnel, and had taken occasion to declare publicly that "he came not over to serve a turn, nor would he act against his conscience." Accordingly he was dismissed, and Tyrconnel brought over with him a ready-made chancellor. One Alexander Fitton, who had been detected in forgery at Westminster and Chester, and fined by the House of Lords, was taken out of prison and made Lord Chancellor of Ireland.[1] His single merit was that he was a convert to Catholicism. A few circumstances of the many related of this judge will give us an idea of his fitness for this great post. He was in the habit of declaring from the bench that all Protestants were rogues, and that amongst forty thousand of them there was not one who was not a traitor, a rebel, and a villain. He overruled the common rules of practice and the law of the land, stating, at the same time, that the Chancery was above all law, and that no law could bind his conscience. After hearing a cause between a Protestant and Roman Catholic, he would say that he would consult a divine, and he would then retire to take the opinion of his chaplain, an ecclesiastic educated in Spain. As assistants to the Chancellor, Dr. Stafford, a priest, and Felix O'Neill, were appointed Masters. To these the causes between Protestants and Roman Catholics were

gentlemen. I shall not need," etc., as above. Clarendon answers for the fact of this address having been delivered.—*Corr.* ii. 56.

[1] Fitton sat in the Dublin Parliament as Lord Gosworth.

generally referred, and upon their report the Chancellor passed his orders and decrees.

In each of the Common Law Courts three judges then sat. Up to 1684 these judges had been Protestants. But when Tyrconnel came into power, two Roman Catholics were at once appointed, and one Protestant retained, "pinioned," as Archbishop King expresses it, by his two brethren. The Protestant "to serve for a pretence of impartiality, and yet to signify nothing," the two Catholics to secure the majority. A Mr. Thomas Nugent, the son of an attainted peer, and who afterwards sat in James's parliament as Lord Riverstown, "who had never been taken notice of at the bar but for more than ordinary brogue and ignorance of the law,"[1] and whom Lord Clarendon calls "a very troublesome, impertinent creature," was made Chief Justice of the King's Bench.[2] The appointment of the son of an attainted person to decide whether the outlawries against his father and others should be reversed, and whether the settlement of the lands should stand, boded no good to the present possessors. Their fears were quickly verified. Nugent, we are told, reversed the outlawries as fast as they came before him. In all the cases between Catholics and Protestants which came into his Court, he was never known, in a single instance, to give judgment for one of the latter. When accused persons were

---

[1] King.
[2] A charge which this judge delivered to the Dublin Grand Jury in 1688 will enable us to form an idea of him. "The Lord Chief Justice Nugent, than whom perhaps the Bench never bore a more confident ignorant Irishman, gave the charge to the Grand Jury, in which he applauded and extolled above the height of an hyperbole the magnanimous and heroic actions of the great and just King James; and on the contrary cast the most vilifying reproaches upon the Prince of Orange. . . . His conclusion was that now the States of Holland were weary of the prince, and that they had sent him over to be dressed as Monmouth was, but that was too good for him. *And that he doubted not before a month passed to hear that they were hung up all over England in bunches like ropes of onions.*"—*Secret Consults*, etc.

acquitted on the palpable perjury of the witnesses for the prosecution, he would not allow the witnesses to be prosecuted, alleging that they had sworn for the king, and that he believed the accused to be guilty, though it could not be proved. He declared from the bench on circuit that rapparees were necessary evils. I shall hereafter call attention to two extravagant decisions of this judge. The other members of this Court were Lyndon, a Protestant, and Sir Brian O'Neal, an inveterate enemy of Englishmen and Protestants.

The Court of Exchequer was then the only one from which there lay no appeal or writ of error into England, and there was therefore no check upon the reversal of outlawries or restraint on decisions contrary to the Acts of Settlement. In consequence the whole business of the kingdom, so far as it related to these matters, and all actions of trespass and ejectment, were brought into this Court. Stephen Rice, an able but intemperate Roman Catholic, was appointed Chief Baron. His hostility to the Acts of Settlement and the Protestant interests was notorious.[1] Before he was made a judge he was often heard to say that he would drive a coach-and-six through these Acts, and before they were repealed by the Irish Parliament which afterwards sat in Dublin he frequently declared on the bench that they were against natural equity, and could not oblige. He used to say from the same place that the Protestants should have nothing from

[1] In the spring of 1688 Nugent and Rice were sent over to England by Tyrconnel with the draft of an Act for the repeal of the Acts of Settlement. Sunderland says that he was offered £40,000 for his concurrence and support. When the matter was first laid before the Privy Council, Lord Bellasis proposed that Nugent and Rice should be committed or commanded to return to Ireland immediately. It was resolved however to hear them. It became known in London that they were the bearers of a proposal to repeal the Acts. On the day they proceeded to the Council their coach was surrounded by boys carrying sticks with potatoes stuck on them, and crying out, "Make room for the Irish ambassadors."—Sunderland's Letter; Harris, *Life of Will. III*, Appen.; *Secret Consults*; *State Tracts*, 3.

him but the utmost rigour of the law. His Court, we are informed, was immediately filled with Papist plaintiffs. "Every one that had a forged deed or a false witness met with favour and countenance from him ; and he, knowing that they could not bring his sentences to England to be examined there, acted as a man that feared no after-account or reckoning. It was before him that all the charters in the kingdom were damned, and that in a term or two, in such a manner that proved him a man of despatch, though not of justice. If he had been left alone, it was really believed that in a few years he would, by some contrivance or other, have given away most of the Protestant estates in Ireland."[1] The companions on the bench of the Chief Baron were Sir Henry Lynch, equally hostile to the Protestants, and Baron Worth,[2] a Protestant.

The Court of Common Pleas was deserted, the business of the kingdom being carried into the King's Bench and the Exchequer. Two of the judges of this Court were able, upright, and honourable men—Keating, the Chief Justice, a Protestant, and Daly, a Roman Catholic. In the correspondence of Lord Clarendon Keating appears as the one dignified character of the letters, and he afterwards showed his worth in the Privy Council before he was dismissed from that

---

[1] King.
[2] Tyrconnel was at one time anxious to remove Worth. Clarendon tells us his opinion of this judge. "Well," said Lord Tyrconnel, "I have only one thing more to say at present, and that is concerning Baron Worth, who, by G——, is a d——d rogue." "How so, my Lord?" said I. "A pox," said he ; "you know he is a Whig, and the greatest favourer of fanatics in the world." On Clarendon's saying that he only knew Worth as a judge, and that he behaved himself as an honest man, Tyrconnel replied, "By G——, I will prove him to be a rogue." "Pray do, my Lord," said Clarendon ; "any charge you bring against him shall be examined." To this Tyrconnel answered, "By G——, I will have it brought to the Council Board. The king has an ill opinion of him, and I will do his business."—Clarendon's *Corr.* i. 457.

body, and by his very noble letter to King James against the repeal of the Acts of Settlement. Daly was also opposed to their repeal, and was afterwards impeached by the Irish Parliament for having said in private that they were not a parliament, but a mere rabble, such as at Naples had thrown up their hats in honour of Massaniello.[1] He was only saved by the sudden joy of the Commons on a false report that Londonderry had surrendered.[2] The third judge was Peter Martin, a Roman Catholic.

4. *The Appointment of Catholic Sheriffs and Justices of the Peace*

Tyrconnel, having remodelled the Courts of Justice to his satisfaction, proceeded to secure to his creatures the execution of the laws and the nomination of juries. In January 1686 Lord Clarendon drew up a list of sheriffs for the following year. He tells us he bestowed particular care in making this list; that before making it he had made inquiries from all

---

[1] Daly was accused of having made use of the following expressions: "That instead of being a parliament, as we pretend, we are more like Massaniello's confused rabble, every man making a noise for an estate and talking nonsense when our lives are in danger; we expect a sudden invasion from England and a bloody war likely to ensue. As persons altogether unmindful of the ruin that hangs over our heads, and without taking any care to prevent it, we are dividing the bear's skin before she is taken. All the honour we do His Majesty is by reflecting on his royal father and brother as wicked and unjust princes, charging them with enacting those laws that were contrary to the laws of God and man."—*True Account of the Present State of Ireland*, London, 1689.

[2] "Tuesday, the 4th instant, we had an alarm that Derry was burnt with bombs, that the king's army had taken it, and put all in it to the sword. Nugent, of Carlandstown, brought this news into the House of Commons just when they were putting to the vote whether they should prosecute the impeachment against Judge Daly. Some think Nugent, being his friend, did it designedly. The news was received with loud huzzas, and in that good and jolly humour they acquitted the judge."—*Letter from Dublin*, 12th June 1689, attached to *The Journal of the Proceedings of the Parliament in Ireland*, 6th July 1689.

persons he could trust, and had taken advice from all quarters respecting the nominations. He was so well satisfied with it that he wrote to Lord Sunderland, " I will venture to say it is the best list of sheriffs that has been for these many years, both for loyalty, prudence, and impartiality." Tyrconnel, however, was not content with this selection of loyal, prudent, and impartial gentlemen. He went over to England, and there, though he had given no intimation in Ireland of his dissatisfaction, and though he was aware who were on the roll before his departure, he complained to the king of Clarendon's selection. The list was sent back to Clarendon with objections, to which he was required to give an answer. The objections were that the gentlemen nominated were Cromwellians or tainted with Whiggism.[1] The objections were satisfactorily answered, and Clarendon's nominees were appointed. But Tyrconnel resolved that none should be appointed for the next year but those of his own way of thinking. He and his creature Nugent, in October 1686, took the extreme step of drawing up a list of those whom they wished to be appointed for the following year, and presented it to the Lord Lieutenant. Clarendon complained of their conduct to the king. In a letter to James, 16th October 1686, he writes: " I humbly beg your Majesty's permission upon this occasion to inform you that the day before my Lord Tyrconnel went hence, he and Mr. Justice Nugent gave me a paper of the names of the persons who were thought to be fit to be sheriffs

---

[1] Tyrconnel mentioned this objection to Lord Clarendon in his usual language. " By G——, my lord, I must needs tell you, the sheriffs you made are generally rogues and old Cromwellians." Lord Clarendon explained the great care he had taken in drawing up the list and ended by saying that " he would justify that these sheriffs, generally speaking, were as good a set of men as any had been chosen these dozen years ; and that he would be judged by the Roman Catholics in any county. To which Tyrconnel answered, " By G——, I believe it, for there has not been an honest man sheriff in Ireland these twenty years."—Clarendon's *Corr.* i. 442.

for the next year. I confess, sir, I thought it very strange, to say no worse of it, for any two men to take upon them to give a list of men for sheriffs over the whole kingdom—to anticipate the representation of the judges, who are the proper persons to offer men fit for those employments, and without so much as leaving room for the Chief Governor to have an opinion in the matter. This list is pretended to be made indifferently of Roman Catholics and Protestants; but I am sure several of them, even of those who are styled Protestants, are men no ways qualified for such offices of trust."[1] The king took no notice of this complaint, and Tyrconnel was allowed to have his way.

Lord Clarendon was right in saying that this list was *pretended* to be made indifferently of Roman Catholics and Protestants. In 1687 there was but one Protestant[2] sheriff appointed in all Ireland, and this one was put in by mistake for another of the same name who was a Catholic. Macaulay has, from contemporary sources, left us a lively picture of these sheriffs. "At the same time the sheriffs, to whom belonged the execution of writs and the nomination of juries, were selected in almost every instance from the caste which had, till very recently, been excluded from all public trusts. It was affirmed that some of these important functionaries had been burned in the hand for theft; others had been servants to Protestants, and the Protestants added, with bitter scorn, that it was fortunate for the country when this was the case, for that a menial who had cleaned the plate and rubbed down the horse of an English gentleman might pass for a civilised being when compared with many of the native aristocracy whose lives had been spent in coshering or marauding." It was so difficult to find Roman Catholics fit to fill this office that many of those appointed for 1687 had to be re-appointed for

---

[1] Clarendon to the king, *Corr.* ii. 36.
[2] Charles Hamilton.

1688. Harris informs us that during these two years not a single instance can be found of a Protestant recovering a debt by execution—"because the poverty of the sheriffs was such that all men were unwilling to trust an execution upon a bond for twenty pounds into their hands, they not being responsible for so small a sum, as many found by too late an experience."[1]

It is to be remembered that Tyrconnel's sheriffs were dispensed from taking the oaths required by law on entering upon their office. Harris, in his edition of Ware's *Writers of Ireland*, tells us how one of these sheriffs was treated by the well-known Charles Leslie,[2] the apologist of King James. The appointment of a disqualified person to the shrievalty of the county of Monaghan alarmed the local gentry. Whereupon they repaired for advice to Leslie, who was then confined by the gout to his house. He told them "that it would be as illegal in them to permit the sheriff to act as it would be in him to attempt it." But they, insisting that Mr. Leslie should appear in person on the bench at the approaching Quarter Sessions, promised that they would all act as he did, and he was carried there in much pain and with much difficulty. Upon inquiry whether the pretended sheriff was legally qualified, he answered pertly "that he was of the

---

[1] "But in plain matters of debt due by bond, or made out by full undeniable ordinance, the judge did commonly grant executions even against Papists; but the matter was so managed with the sheriff that the debtor might go publicly about his affairs in spite of the decrees or executions against him in the hands of the sheriff, who would be sure to avoid him upon all occasions. I should be extreme tedious . . . if I should here give an account of all the oppressions and unjust proceedings of this kind to which I was myself a witness."—*A Short View*, etc., London, 1689.

[2] Clarendon thus speaks of this gentleman: "I shall take it for a very great favour if you will bestow the Chancellorship of Connor upon Mr. Charles Lesley, a man of good parts, admirable learning, an excellent preacher, and of an incomparable life."—*Corr.* i. 405. Leslie was appointed Chancellor of Connor in 1687.

king's own religion, and that it was His Majesty's will that he should be sheriff." Mr. Leslie replied "that they were not inquiring into His Majesty's religion, but whether he had qualified himself according to law for acting as a proper officer; that the law was the king's will, and nothing else to be deemed such; that his subjects had no other way of knowing his will but as it is revealed to them in his laws, and it must always be thought to continue so, till the contrary is notified to them in the same authentic manner." Wherefore the Bench unanimously agreed to commit the pretended sheriff for his intrusion and arrogant contempt of the Court.[1]

That the same interest might be predominant in every part of the kingdom, the commissions of the peace underwent a similar regulation. It is true that some few Protestants were continued in it; but they were rendered useless and insignificant, being overpowered by the great number of natives joined with them, and "those, for the most part, of the very scum of the people, and a great many whose fathers had been executed for theft, robbery, or murder."[2] So little regard was had to character that a man was appointed chief magistrate in a northern city who had been condemned to the gallows for his crimes.[3] Of one of these justices I have already spoken—the gentleman who stated from the bench that all the rogues and vagabonds of the country had been swept into the new-modelled army.

5. *The Attack on the Corporations*

But however large these strides were, they fell short of the projects of Tyrconnel and his party. Speedily as the forfeitures were being reversed, and the land restored to the natives, they were not satisfied. He and they aimed at the

---

[1] Ware's *Works*, edition of 1764.
[2] Harris.   [3] Burdy.

total extirpation of the English interest by means of an Irish Parliament. The corporations, about a hundred in number, were in the hands of the Protestants, and these bodies enjoyed the right of sending representatives to the legislature. Tyrconnel, having secured the appointment of native returning officers in the counties, turned his attention to the towns. All the corporate towns of Ireland, with the exception of Dublin, Limerick, Waterford, and Cork, which had been built by the Danes, had been founded by the English settlers at their own cost and charge to be the strongholds of their interest. Thirty of them had been built in the reign of James I. alone,[1] and almost every householder in them was a Protestant. The first attempt was made on the Corporation of Dublin. Tyrconnel, then Lord Deputy, sent for the Lord Mayor and aldermen, and asked them to surrender their charter, stating that the king had resolved to call in all the charters in the country in order to enlarge their privileges, and that His Majesty expected their ready compliance. To this request it was answered that a common council would be called, and the matter laid before it. This was done, and the Mayor was authorised to tell the Deputy that the rights and privileges of the corporation were secured by one hundred and thirty charters, and to pray him that their ancient government should be continued to them. Tyrconnel, as usual with him, fell into a tempest of passion, rated them soundly for their rebellion, and told them to go their ways and resolve to obey, lest a worse thing should befall them.[2] Overwhelmed by these menaces and reproaches, the Mayor called another council; but the members persisted unanimously in refusing to surrender their charters. To qualify the refusal a deputation proceeded to the castle to acquaint Tyrconnel with the reasons for their refusal, and to pray for time to petition the king, who, on a former occa-

[1] Harris.   [2] Ralph.

sion, had acknowledged their eminent sufferings for his royal father, and assured them that he would reward them therefor. With this acknowledgment and promise Tyrconnel was now made acquainted, but without effect. He commenced to storm as before, and said that instead of writing in their favour to the king he would write against them.[1] A *quo warranto* was immediately issued against the corporation. The case came on before Chief Baron Rice in the Exchequer, into which Court this and all the subsequent *quo warrantos* were brought, to prevent writs of error into England. The corporation was not allowed as much time to put in their plea as was necessary to transcribe it. A date being mistaken by the clerk in one of their charters (we have seen that they had a hundred and thirty), the corporation prayed leave to amend it. Leave was refused, and judgment was given against them. The fate which befell the corporation of the capital was that of all the corporations in the country. Within the short space of two terms—such was the despatch of Tyrconnel's judges—the charters of all the corporations in the kingdom were forfeited or superseded.

New charters were granted; but by these new charters the corporations were made absolute slaves to the caprice of the Lord Deputy. A clause was inserted in all of them empowering Tyrconnel to put in and turn out whom he pleased without trial or reason shown. In filling up the new corporations it was the general rule that two-thirds of the members should be Catholics and one-third Protestants. The Protestants declined to serve at all. Of the Catholics appointed many never saw the town for which they were named, nor were concerned in trade; some were named for several corporations; most of them were in indigent circumstances.[2] The case of one illustrious town will explain to us the sweeping changes wrought throughout the kingdom.

[1] Ralph.   [2] Harris.

The charter of Londonderry[1] had been declared forfeited, and its corporation remodelled. Among its new aldermen and burgesses, sixty-five in number, twenty were Protestants and forty-five were Roman Catholics.[2]

6. *Remodelling of the Privy Council*

The Privy Council in Ireland at this time had duties, and acted a part in the constitution which was not performed by the Privy Council in England. No proposed Act could be introduced into the Irish Legislature until the Lord Lieutenant and his council had certified the causes and reasons for it. It became necessary, therefore, to remodel this body also. A large number of Roman Catholics were introduced, or rather drafted into it, for some who were named for it were either ashamed or unwilling to accept the honour. In May 1686 twenty new members were added, of whom eighteen were Roman Catholics. Two were Protestants,

---

[1] "The same being done in all other corporations either by voluntary resignation or a short trial, more for form than with design to avoid it, it cost no great trouble except at Londonderry (a stubborn people as they appeared afterwards), who stood an obstinate suit, but were forced at last to undergo the same fate with the rest."—Clarke's *James II.*

[2] Macaulay is mistaken in saying that there was only one person of Anglo-Saxon extraction in the new-modelled corporation. He was misled by two lines in the "Londeriados," a poem written between the years 1695-99—

"In all the corporation not a man
Of *British* parents except Buchanan."

Among the names of the new corporators are to be found Manby, Dobbin, Hamilton, Burnside, Lecky, Stanley, Gordon, etc.—Hempton, *Siege and History of Londonderry*. The "Londeriados" informs us of the class from which the new members were chosen—

"For burgesses and freemen they had chose
Brogue-makers, butchers, raps, and such as those."

This poem is to be found in Hempton. When the corporation was new modelled, its plate was wisely hidden until better times.

and one of them, Lord Granard, who had been deprived of his regiment in the remodelling of the army, was appointed President of the Council, an office until then unknown in Ireland.[1] Lord Granard declined to act. In fact, all the Protestant lords ceased to attend, "since they were so vastly outnumbered as to prevent their doing either the Protestants or their country service."[2]

Thus was the whole military, civil, and administrative power in the country transferred to the native Irish. The transference was undertaken by Tyrconnel with a light heart; but the cost of the operation was the ruin of the English settlers and the desolation of the kingdom. The first steps of Tyrconnel—the disarming of the Protestants, and their exclusion from the army—had alarmed the settlers, and stirred up against them an excitable and hostile population. I have already spoken of the fatal consequences of these proceedings. When it became known that Tyrconnel had been appointed Lord Deputy[3] the alarm became universal, and the exodus of the English assumed a proportionate magnitude. Every Protestant who was able withdrew himself and his family to England or Scotland.[4] So anxious were men to be gone that they tempted the dangers of the Irish Sea in skiffs and open boats. When Lord Clarendon relin-

---

[1] "For there never was a President of the Council here before; and the statute takes no notice of, nor appoints a place for such an office here, as it does in England."—Clarendon's *Corr.* i. 417.

[2] Harris.

[3] "The confirmation of this dismal news reaching the ears of the Protestants in Ireland struck like a thunderbolt. Perhaps no age or story can parallel so dreadful a catastrophe among all ages and sexes as if the day of doom was come; every one lamenting the dreadfulness of their horrible condition, and almost all that could by any means deserted the kingdom if they had but money to discharge their passage. A demonstration of this were those infinite numbers of families which flocked over from Dublin to the Isle of Man and other places."—*Secret Consults*, etc.

[4] Among the refugees of 1687 was the celebrated William Molyneux.

quished the Government in 1687 to Tyrconnel, fifteen hundred families left Ireland with him. During the first year of Tyrconnel's administration the evils increased and the condition of the country became still more deplorable. Lamentable as this state was in 1687, the sufferings became greater when in the winter of the following year the army was increased. Fifty thousand[1] Irish troops, ill-disciplined and hostile to the Protestants, were let loose on the country. At the same time large bodies of the peasantry collected and ravaged the land unchecked. What few effects had been left to the unfortunate Protestants were at once swept away.[2] "The destruction of property which took place within a few weeks," says Macaulay, "would be incredible if it were not attested by witnesses unconnected with each other and attached to very different interests. There is a close and sometimes almost a verbal agreement between the descriptions given by Protestants who, during that reign of terror, escaped at the hazard of their lives to England, and the descriptions given by the envoys, commissaries, and captains of Lewis. All agreed in declaring that it would take many years to repair the waste which had been wrought in a few weeks by the armed peasantry. The French ambassador reported to his master that in six weeks 50,000 horned cattle had been slain, and were rotting on the ground all over the country. The number of sheep that were butchered during the same time was popularly said to have been three or four hundred thousand."[3]

[1] This is the lowest calculation. Ranke says: "Nach den geringsten Angaben wohlunterrichteter betrug sie doch 50,000 man."
[2] Keating's letter to King James in Append. of King.
[3] This estimate is much below that of the refugee Protestants. One of them describes these ravages as follows: "And, to be short, the spoil was so general and great that in December and part of January last they had destroyed in the counties of Cork and Kerry above four thousand head of black cattle, as cows and oxen, and there and in the county of Tipperary two or three hundred thousand sheep. And so in all

A patriotic eye-witness has left us two pictures of the country which bring into glaring contrast the past and the then present state of Ireland, and disclose the former prosperity and the latter desolation. Chief-Justice Keating, "whom all parties will own to be a good man,"[1] in his celebrated letter to King James, in May 1689, tells him how Ireland—"from the most improved and improving spot of earth in Europe; from stately herds and flocks; from plenty of money at 7 or 8 per cent, whereby trade and industry were encouraged, and all upon the security of those Acts of Parliament; from great and convenient buildings newly erected in cities and other corporations, to that degree that even the city of Dublin is, since the passing of these Acts, and the security and quiet promised from them, enlarged to double what it was; and the shipping in divers ports were five or six times more than ever was known before, to the vast increase of your Majesty's revenue"—was reduced "to the saddest and most disconsolate condition of any kingdom or country in Europe." The same judge, who remembered what the country had been only four years before, lamented at the Assizes[2] at Wicklow, in language of extraordinary earnestness and force, the miseries of the kingdom. He told the Grand Jury that a great part of the island was devastated by a rabble armed with unusual weapons: "I mean half-pikes and skeans; I must tell you plainly it looks rather like a design to massacre and murder than anything else.

other parts, especially the provinces of Munster and Leinster proportionably; so that before the beginning of February it was thought they had destroyed in all parts of the kingdom above one million head of cattle, besides corn and houses, and thereby utterly spoiled the most plentiful country in these parts of Europe; so that twenty years of perfect peace cannot be thought to restore it to the state in which it was at the death of King Charles the Second."—*Ireland's Lamentation*, 1689; see also *A Short View*, etc., 1689.

[1] Clarendon.
[2] *State Trials*, xii. 615, 635.

I am told that open markets are set up in this county—a fat bullock for five shillings and a fat sheep for one shilling. Under the old law the Jews were not to seethe the kid in the mother's milk; but these unmerciful wretches go further than that, sparing none, but destroying old and young. It would make every honest man's heart to bleed to hear what I have heard since I came into this county. It is ill in other parts of the country; but here they spare not even the wearing clothes and habits of women and children, that they are forced to come abroad naked without anything to cover their nakedness; so that besides the oath you have taken, and the obligation of Christianity that lies upon you as Christians, I conjure you by all that is sacred, and as ever you expect eternal salvation, that you make diligent inquiry." In a subsequent case at the same Assizes he renewed his complaint. "There are such general and vast depredations in the country that many honest men go to bed possessed of considerable stocks of black and white cattle, gotten by great labour and pains, the industry of their whole lives, and in the morning when they arise not anything left them, but, burned out of all, to go a begging, all being taken away by rebels, thieves, and robbers, the sons of violence. On this side the Cape of Good Hope, where are the most brutish and barbarous people we read of, there is none like the people of this country, nor so great a desolation as in this kingdom. It is come to that pass, that a man that loses the better part of his substance chooses rather to let that, and what he has besides, go, than come to give evidence. And why? Because he is certain to have his house burnt and his throat cut if he appears against them. Good God, what a pass are we come to!" In reading these descriptions and lamentations it must never be forgotten that up to this time, and long afterwards, all Ireland south of Dublin was peaceful and free from the ravages of war; yet the country had been changed into a wilderness by the devastations of the peasantry and the connivance of Tyrconnel's government.

The Protestants computed their losses during these four years of misgovernment at eight millions of money.[1] Macaulay points out that all such estimates must be inexact. "We are not, however, absolutely without materials for such an estimate. The Quakers were neither a very numerous nor a very opulent class. We can hardly suppose that they were more than a fiftieth part of the Protestant population, or that they possessed more than a fiftieth part of the Protestant wealth of Ireland. They were, undoubtedly, better treated than any other Protestant sect. James had always been partial to them.[2] They own that Tyrconnel did his best to protect them, and they seem to have found favour even in the sight of the rapparees. Yet the Quakers computed their pecuniary losses at a hundred thousand pounds." If we take into consideration what must have been spared to the Quakers by the protection of Tyrconnel and the favour of the rapparees, the estimate of their losses by the general body of the Protestants will not appear to be exaggerated.

---

[1] *Vindication of the Protestants of Ireland*, 1689; *Character of the Protestants of Ireland*, 1689.

[2] The Quakers were certainly well affected to James and were in consequence favoured by him. When Dykvelt came over to England in 1687 he succeeded in reconciling all the nonconformists, except this body, to the interest of William.—Mazure's *Histoire de la Révolution*, iii. 11. Quakers were introduced as numerously as their small numbers allowed, into the remodelled corporations in Ireland, and two, Anthony Sharp and Samuel Clarrage, were made aldermen of Dublin, and excused from the oaths.—*Ireland's Lamentation*. Story informs us "they say it was a Quaker that first proposed this invention of brass money; but whoever it was, they did that party a signal piece of service, since they would never have been able to have carried on the war without it. However, the Quakers have been very serviceable to that interest, for I am assured by some in the Irish army that they maintained a regiment at their own cost, besides several presents of value that they made to the late king."—*Impartial History*, p. 50.

SECTION III

THE PARLIAMENT OF 1689

JAMES landed at Kingsale on the 12th of March 1689, and on the 14th proceeded to Cork, where he commenced to act as a king. He created Tyrconnel a duke, and issued an edict against exporting wool to England, while giving a general liberty for sending it to France.[1] From Cork he rode to Dublin, which he reached on the 24th.[2] From St. James's Gate, the one by which he entered, he was conducted to the Castle by the Lord Mayor and aldermen, the judges and State officers, and a muster of about twenty coaches. The sword of State was carried by Tyrconnel immediately before James, who was mounted on a "padnag in a plain cinnamon-coloured cloth suit and black slouching hat, and a George hung over his shoulder with a blue ribbon."[3] On his arrival at the gate of the castle he was met by the host, covered by a canopy borne by four bishops, accompanied by a numerous train of friars singing. On seeing this procession James immediately dismounted and fell on his knees to receive a blessing from the Roman Catholic primate, who was present. He

---

[1] *Life of James II.*, written by himself; Macpherson's *Original Papers*, i. 176.

[2] "It was impossible for the king to proceed immediately to Dublin, for the southern counties had been so completely laid waste by the banditti whom the priests had called to arms that the means of locomotion were not easily to be procured. Horses had become rarities; in a large district there were only two carts, and those D'Avaux pronounced good for nothing."—MACAULAY.

[3] *Ireland's Lamentation*, being a short account, etc., 1689.

then rose and passed into the castle, from which a banner waved with this inscription on it, *Now or never; now and for ever.*[1]

The next morning he called a council, and having first erased from its list the names of Lord Granard and Chief-Justice Keating, he ordered five proclamations to be issued,—(1) for raising the value of the currency;[2] (2) summoning a parliament for the 7th of May following; (3) requiring all who had left the kingdom to return with assurance of protection; (4) commending his Roman Catholic subjects for having armed themselves, yet "whereas it had encouraged some certain robberies," ordering all who were not in the army to lay up their weapons in their houses; (5) enacting the carriage of provisions to the army in the North, and forbidding his soldiers and officers from seizing any without payment.

Some writers have expressed the opinion that, although James during his stay in Ireland was not a king *de jure*, yet that he ought to be considered as a king *de facto*. James never was a king *de facto* of or in Ireland.[3] A king *de facto* is one who is in peaceable possession of a kingdom, though a flaw in his title may exist, or be afterwards discovered. When James landed in Ireland the entire north was in possession of those who disputed his title and had transferred their allegiance to William. During the whole period of his stay in Ireland James was strictly a militant challenger. The only claim which James ever had to the crown of Ireland was in right of his English crown. By the statute law of Ireland the Irish crown was inseparably annexed to that of England, and the possessor of the latter became at once

---

[1] *Apology for the Irish Protestants; State Tracts*, 3.

[2] A guinea was raised to twenty-four shillings; an English shilling to thirteenpence; a ducatoon from 6s. to 6s. 3d.; a cob from 4s. 9d. to 5s.; a French louis to 19s.—*Ireland's Lamentation*, etc.

[3] Plowden says in his *Review* that James continued to be after his flight from England both *de jure* and *de facto* king of Ireland. But Plowden's opinions and facts are of about equal value. Charles O'Conor justly accuses him of misrepresentation and ignorance of Irish history.

and *ipso facto* entitled to the crown of Ireland. Upon the transfer of the English crown, in whatever manner it was effected, the transferee became at once, and without any action of the Irish Parliament, the rightful sovereign of Ireland. If James had forfeited the crown of England—a position which cannot be questioned, inasmuch as our whole constitution is based upon it—he had no right whatever, when he arrived in Ireland, to the crown of that country.[1] He was an adventurer, and exactly in the position of Lambert Simnel who was crowned in Dublin, except that James had once been the lawful sovereign of Ireland. It follows from this that James was incapable of summoning an Irish parliament. But this was not the only illegality which tainted the assembly called by him. By the law of Ireland no parliament could be called without a warrant under the Great Seal of England certifying the laws which were to be passed, and permitting the meeting of the legislative body. No doubt these considerations did not influence the lower orders of Irish who flocked to James's standard, and who were acquainted with no law except that of their native impulse. But there was not a member of James's council, nor of the Dublin assembly, that did not know that the Parliament was summoned by one who had no right to call it, and that it was an act of treason to sit in it or to take a part in its proceedings.

James was now among subjects from whom he was to experience nothing but slights, insults, and open opposition to the *new* policy which he had determined to adopt in Ireland. There was already, though as yet unknown to either party, a growing incompatibility between the views of James and those of his Irish supporters who were bent on the restoration of the land to its former owners and the separation of Ireland from Great Britain. James had lately, under the advice of Louis XIV, modified his former inten-

---

[1] The crown of England was offered to and accepted by William and Mary on the 13th of February 1689.

tion of an immediate repeal of the Acts of Settlement. The French king had recommended him to defer this project till he had repossessed himself of the English throne, and in the meantime to reconcile the Irish Protestants to his interests.[1] In 1687 James and Tyrconnel had an interview at Chester, and there it was agreed between them to proceed at once with the repeal of the Acts of Settlement and with the consequent confiscation of the estates of the Protestants.[2] But when this resolution was adopted James was still king; subsequent events had wrought a change in his views. Every reason was in favour of the deceitful and disingenuous policy which was recommended by Louis. It would have pleased the party of James in England; its tendency was to lessen the opposition of the Protestants of Ireland. The repeal of the Acts of Settlement was viewed unfavourably by the vast majority of the English Jacobites, even by the Roman Catholics of that party; and James was well assured that if he pronounced for the independence of Ireland, England would never forgive the king who had declared for such a measure. The circumstances of Ireland lent additional weight to the advice of Louis. If ever a man was bound to conciliate the Protestants of Ireland it was James. He was well aware that all the wealth and resources of the island were in their possession, and that nothing would strengthen the hands of his English and Scotch friends, and allay the suspicions entertained of him, so much as justice and kindness to the Irish Protestants. It would have been a complete answer to his enemies if he could have shown that in

[1] Ranke, *History of England*, iv. 536, translation.
[2] "Pendant ce voyage, my lord Tyrconnel s'etoit rendu a Chester aupres du Roi et prit les ordres sur l'Irlande. Un mois après, Barillon annoncoit a Louis XIV la resolution de renverser ce que l'on nommoit l'etablissment, c'est-a-dire, de rendre aux Irlandois les biens dont ils avoient ete depossedés sous la republique. Cet etablissment avoit eté confirme a la restauration." "Les mesures," desoit Barillon, "sont prises pour en venir a bout."—Mazure, *La Révolution de* 1688, ii. 286.

Ireland, where he was supported by the majority, he had not only abstained from ill-treating the Protestants, but had on the contrary protected and supported them. James saw that his interests demanded the conciliation of the Irish Protestants, and that a policy of amnesty and mildness would strengthen his claims and increase his chances of restoration.[1] His aim was to recover his British throne either by means of a peaceful recall or by an invasion. Ireland was regarded by him merely as a stepping-stone to that end. It was of the highest importance to him not to offend his English friends by throwing Ireland into confusion, or to renew their fears by oppressing the Irish Protestants. On the other hand, if it should become necessary to invade England, and to encourage his supporters there by an imposing display of force, it was to the Irish army that he could look for success in his undertaking. He could neither make use of that army, nor even keep it together, if he placed himself in opposition to the wishes of those who raised and maintained it.[2] The French friends who accompanied James into Ireland joined the Irish party, and were of opinion that his only hope of safety lay in throwing himself heart and soul into the views of the extreme Irish faction; while Melfort and his English councillors recommended the conciliation of the Protestants. James's private wishes were undoubtedly in favour of restoring the lands to the native Irish. Yet he could not but see in his lucid moments that a general con-

---

[1] Ranke tells us that a proclamation, assuring the Protestants of the restoration to their estates and of their admission to public offices, was actually drawn up by order of James after his arrival in Ireland, but that its publication was prevented by the Irish and French factions.

[2] The Irish army was not paid till after the arrival of James. He himself mentions this, "for the troops being raised and having no pay, were forced to live on the people; and though the officers had undertaken to maintain them at their own charge, there were very few that did it effectually."—*Life of James II*, written by himself; Macpherson's *Original Papers*, i. 176.

fiscation would injure his prospects. But James discovered that it was easier to excite hopes than to arrest them at maturity. He and Tyrconnel had been working for years for the repeal of the Acts of Settlement, and he was now carried away by the flood the gates of which he had himself opened. The underhand shifts and vacillations to which he was forced by his present desire to conciliate the Protestants, and at the same time to retain the affections of his Irish allies, were pitiable. He would and he would not, one day exhorting the Protestant bishops to oppose the repeal of the Acts of Settlement, the next urging on their revocation more speedily than it would otherwise have gone. At the very time when he was secretly encouraging the Protestant peers[1] to oppose in every way their repeal, the following scene took place in the House of Lords, which James attended every day. On the 28th of May a motion was made for adjourning over a holiday. "The king asked, 'What holiday?' Answered, 'the restoration of his brother and himself.' He replied, 'the fitter to restore those loyal Catholic gentlemen who had suffered with him and been kept unjustly out of their estates.' The motion rejected."[2]

But the recovery of his other kingdoms by James was a matter of the smallest importance to the vindictive and improvident men who now had him in their power. They saw, or thought they saw, for there was not one of them gifted with a particle of political foresight or wisdom, a propitious opportunity for carrying into effect their extravagant schemes.

[1] "I appeal to the Earl of Granard whether Duke Powis did not give him thanks from King James for the opposition he made in the House of Lords to the passing the Act of Attainder and the Act for repeal of the Acts of Settlement, and desired that he and the other Protestant lords should use their endeavours to obstruct them. To which the Lord Granard answered that they were too few to effect that; but if the king would not have them pass, his way was to engage some of the Roman Catholic lords to stop them. To which the duke replied with an oath that the king durst not let them know that he had a mind to have them stopt."—Leslie's *Answer to King*, p. 99.

[2] *Journal of the proceedings in the Irish Parliament*, 1689.

They quickly took the measure of James and discovered what a king of shreds and patches had come among them.[1] Encouraged by the internal troubles of Great Britain, and resolved to carry out their plans of confiscation and proscription, they made use of James and of his title of king solely for their own purposes, and compelled him to renounce his policy of conciliation, and in so doing to consummate his own ruin and that of his family.[2] Now that they had the whole power of the kingdom in their hands, they threw moderation and all thoughts of the future to the winds.[3] They made what was virtually a declaration of war against England and the English interest in Ireland, while at the same time they gave a dreadful note of warning respecting the treatment which awaited the Protestants of Ireland in case they should remain masters of the country. The object of the Irish party was the threefold one which is sure to make its appearance in every Irish agitation, whatever may

---

[1] On the 18th of May, in the midst of their preparations for confiscation and proscription, the Irish around James sent to England, without his knowledge as he tells us, and published there a proclamation in his name, declaring that the Protestants were living under James in the greatest freedom, quiet, and security both as to their properties and religion. Some Scotch officers who, in the winter of 1689, came over to Dublin, said that if their countrymen had known how the Protestants had been treated in Ireland not a man of them would have fought for James. This proclamation is to be found in *Parliamentary History*, v. 303 ; and in Clarke's *Life of James*, ii. 362.

[2] Speaking of the Acts to which he was obliged by his Irish allies to consent, James says "nothing but his unwillingness to disgust those who were otherwise affectionate subjects could have extorted [this consent] from him. It had without doubt been more generous in the Irish not to have pressed so hard upon their prince when he lay so much at their mercy, and more prudent not to have grasped at regaining all before they were sure of keeping what they already possessed."—Clarke's *Life*, ii. 361.

[3] "But the Irish, by reckoning themselves sure of their game, when in reality they had the worse of it, thought of nothing but settling themselves in riches and plenty by breaking the Act of Settlement, and by that means raise new enemies before they were secure of mastering those they had already on their hands."—James's words, *ib*. ii. 354.

have been its commencement,—Roman Catholic ascendency, separation from Great Britain, and the possession of the land. The first the Irish had already obtained by the means I have mentioned. They were now about to make their final and fatal attempt to attain the latter two. Tyrconnel and his party had been for four years making their preparations for a Parliament which should fully carry out Irish ideas. The hour was now come, and in May 1689 a Parliament assembled in Dublin which has ever since been to all impartial men who are acquainted with its proceedings a world's wonder.

This parliament met on the 7th of May and continued its sittings till the 20th of July following. I have already pointed out the double illegality which attached to it; that it was summoned by one who had no right to call it, and that it sat directly in the teeth of Poynings' law.[1] The constitution of this assembly was peculiar. Out of ninety Protestant lords only five temporal peers and four bishops attended. Ten Roman Catholic peers had obeyed the writ of summons; but by the reversal of old attainders and new creations, seventeen more, all Roman Catholics, were introduced into the house. Of the twenty-four Catholics who generally attended, fifteen had had their attainders reversed, and four were minors. No Roman Catholic prelates were summoned. This was greatly against the wish of the Parliament, which desired that all the Protestant bishops should be excluded, and Roman Catholics summoned in their place.[2] It was the work of the king, who still hoped that some moderation would be observed, and encouraged the Protestant bishops in their attendance and opposition to the repeal of the Acts of Settlement.

---

[1] Yet Poynings' law was not repealed by this Parliament. A Bill to that effect was introduced into the Commons, but on James expressing his dissatisfaction the Bill was allowed to drop.—KING.

[2] "Diese Versammlung missbilligte, dass die Protestanischen Bischöfe nicht mit einem Schlage entfernt, und Catholische an ihre Stelle gesetzt wurden."—RANKE.

This conduct of James was remarked with dislike, and he was accused of being an Englishman, and of showing too much lenity to the Protestants. A Roman Catholic author and actor in these scenes tells us that the king's conduct in the temple showed him to be a good Catholic, but his conduct in the senate proved him to be a Protestant.[1]

The House of Commons then consisted of three hundred members, elected by the freeholders in counties, and by the burgesses in corporations. Tyrconnel took care to pack this house with his creatures. We have seen how the sheriffs of counties and the corporations had been secured.[2] To make certain that none but safe men should be returned, letters were sent with the writs recommending the persons whom Tyrconnel wished to be elected. Upon the receipt of these letters the sheriff or magistrate assembled such as he thought fit, and these, without making any noise about it, made a return, so that the Protestants either did not know of the election, or were afraid to appear at it.[3] Two hundred and thirty-two members were returned. Six only were Protest-

---

[1] "James, however, was so intent upon following the advice of his favourites, not to act anything in favour of the Irish or for the re-establishment of the worship of Rome that might dissatisfy his Protestant subjects in England [who, as they believed, would undoubtedly recall him if he continued his wonted moderation], that pursuant to this maxim, he would not admit the Roman Catholic bishops to take their places in the Assembly of the States, though he allowed it to four Protestant bishops, all the rest of that stamp being gone into England to join with William, and these also declared for him as soon as he appeared with any power in Ireland. So that whoever considers the different behaviour of this prince in the temple and senate would take him for a serious Roman Catholic in the one, and a true Protestant in the other."—Colonel Kelly, *Macariæ Excidium*.

[2] When the elections took place few of the new charters to the corporations had passed the seal.—*List of the Lords Spiritual and Temporal*, etc., 1689. In the *Secret Consults*, published 1690, it is stated "most of the new charters are yet in the Attorney General's hands for want of paying the fees, and the several corporations act without them."

[3] Harris, *Life of Will. III*.

ants.[1] Thirty-four[2] boroughs and counties were not represented.

It was a Parliament so summoned and so constituted that proceeded to pass Acts "which seem to have been framed by madmen."[3] The king, in his opening speech, had referred in cautious terms to the Acts of Settlement. After stating that he was "against invading any man's property," he proceeded, "I shall most readily consent to the making of such good, wholesome laws as may be for the good of the nation, the improvement of trade, and relieving such as have been injured by the late Acts of Settlement, so far forth as may be consistent with reason, justice, and the public good." These words have been tortured into an attack on these Acts; but nothing was further from James's thought than their present repeal. Some hard cases had undoubtedly occurred on the former settlement of the nation, and it was the king's wish that a sum of money should be set apart to indemnify the sufferers,[4] or that a compromise between the old and present proprietors should be effected. But such moderation was

---

[1] Of these six two, Sir John Mead and Joseph Coghlan, members for the University, opposed the repeal of the Acts of Settlement, and finding that they could do no good, retired from the House.—*List of the Lords*, etc., 1689.

[2] Harris.

[3] Dalrymple.

[4] James tells us in his Memoirs: "It is certain that many of the wise and judicious Catholics thought such an accommodation very practicable; that the great improvements had so enhanced the value of most estates as would allow the old proprietors a share of equal income to what their ancestors lost, and yet leave a competency for the purchasers, who might reasonably be allowed the benefit of their own labours. And in such turbulent times and difficult circumstances it was just that all pretenders should recede in some degree from the full of their pretensions for the accommodation of the whole; no side being so apt to grumble when all men share the burden, especially it being of that consequence to prevent a universal discontent, both for the king's present necessities, the public quiet and general safety of the people. There is no doubt but the king's inclinations were the same."—Clarke's *Life*, ii. 358.

hateful to the Irish. A Bill for repealing the Acts of Settlement was brought in by Chief-Justice Nugent, and received with a hurrah, "which more resembled the behaviour of a crew of rapparees over a rich booty than that of a senate appointed to rectify abuses, and restore the rights of their fellow-subjects."[1] James did his best to prevent the Bill passing. He even threatened to dissolve the Parliament. But his expostulations and remonstrances only irritated the Irish against him. They said openly that if he did not give them back the land they would not fight for him. Even the soldiers in the streets shouted the same thing after him as he passed by.[2] James still resisted, and at the last moment resolved on a dissolution. But his evil genius,[3] D'Avaux, stood beside him. The united Irish and French factions were too strong for James alone and unsupported. He yielded. "Alas!" said the unfortunate king, "I am fallen into the hands of people who will ram that and much more down my throat."

A general[4] in the service of James was asked, a few months later, how it was that the king had consented to the Act of Attainder and the repeal of the Acts of Settlement. " Sir," was the answer, "if you did but know the circumstances the king is under, and the hardships these men put upon him, you would bemoan him with tears instead of blaming him. What would you have him do? All his other subjects have

---

[1] Ralph.

[2] Ranke; Leslie. The king was "at the same time as good as told underhand, that if he consented not to it, the whole nation would abandon him."—James's words, Clarke's *Life*, ii. 360.

[3] Macaulay says, "it is not too much to say that of the difference between right and wrong Avaux had no more notion than a brute." It was D'Avaux who proposed to James a general massacre of the Protestants if an army should land from England. "Qu'ainsi j'etois d'avis," wrote the unconscious scoundrel, "qu'apres que la descente etant fait, si on apprenoit que de Protestans se fussent soulevés en quelque endroit du royaume, on fit main basse sur tous generalment."
—Quoted by Ranke.

[4] Major-General Maxwell, a Roman Catholic.

deserted him; this is the only body of men he has now to appear for him; he is in their hands, and must please them."[1]

James was obliged to yield. The Acts of Settlement were repealed, and twelve millions of acres were transferred to the Irish.[2] The original Act of Settlement had been confirmed by two subsequent Acts and many patents, both of Charles and James. The Lords Lieutenant, and judges on their circuits, had been repeatedly ordered to proclaim the settled resolution of these princes to maintain them. Trusting to the Acts and these frequent declarations, the proprietors had reared stately buildings and carried out extensive improvements and reclamations of the soil. Seats had been erected and parks enclosed. Many of the estates had passed into the hands of purchasers for valuable consideration. Manufactories had been established in divers places, "whereby the meanest inhabitants were at once enriched and civilised; it would hardly be believed it were the same spot of earth."[3] Thousands had sold small estates and freeholds in England,[4] and laid out their prices in Irish land. Purchases, settlements, leases, money investments, jointures for widows, and portions for children—all the multifarious dispositions of property required by society for the welfare of families, for its trade and commerce, or the reclamation, improvement, and adornment of the soil—had been made on the faith of these Acts and an undisputed possession of many years. All these were now swept away at one stroke, without compensation or provision for the unhappy sufferers. James alone manifested compassion for these unfortunates. To make some compensation for the evil inflicted against his will, he gave ten thousand pounds a year out of his own estate.

Well might Chief-Justice Keating indignantly ask:

[1] Leslie, p. 100.
[2] Even the son of Sir Phelim O'Neill was restored to the estate of which his father was so justly deprived.
[3] Keating. [4] Ib.

"Where or when shall a man purchase in this kingdom? Under what title or on what security shall he lay out his money, or secure the portions he designs for his children, if he may not do it under the security of divers Acts of Parliament, the solemn and reiterated declarations of his prince, and a quiet and uninterrupted possession of twenty years together? And this is the case of thousands of families who are purchasers under the Acts of Settlement and Explanations."

Lest some owners of land should be forgotten, or not included in the sweeping net of this Act, a clause was added whereby the property of all those who dwelt or stayed in any part of the three kingdoms which did not acknowledge James, or who aided or corresponded with such since the 1st of August 1688, was declared to be forfeited. There had been for some time a constant and lively correspondence between Ireland and England and between the rest of Ireland and the north. So that every one who had been in England or the north of Ireland after the 1st August 1688, and every one who corresponded with any such persons, lost his estate. By a strain of severity at once ridiculous and detestable, almost every Protestant in Ireland who could write was to be deprived of his estate.[1] Nor was this a mere threat. Mr. Lecky says that these words would, if strictly construed, comprehend all Irish proprietors who were living peacefully in England, or who had written on private business to any one residing in a part of the kingdom which acknowledged William. But he thinks they were intended to include those only who had taken an active part against James. Nugent, Tyrconnel's Chief-Justice of the King's Bench, entertained no such doubts as to the effect of these words. This judge decided that accepting and paying a bill of exchange was a correspondence with the enemies of King James. And in another case, where an attorney had received letters from clients asking him to

[1] Leland.

apply for a reprieve of sentence for them, Nugent held that this also was a correspondence with the enemy, and imprisoned the attorney on a charge of high treason.

The same author has been courageous enough to assert that compensation for some of the despoiled owners was provided in this Act of Repeal. No statement could be more directly in opposition to the facts of the case. If compensation means an equivalent for property taken away, and that is the only meaning which the word bears in the English language, there was no compensation for any class. It is true that the Act speaks of compensation, but all that is contained in the enactment is a mere conditional promise to be fulfilled, if ever, in the future, and even that is limited to one class, namely purchasers. All who derived from the original grantees by descent, by devise, or by marriage, far the greater number, were absolutely excluded. It is a strange use of language to call such a partial and ineffectual provision compensation, and to give to the mere shadow the name of the substance. But when we come to examine the so-called compensation to purchasers we find it a mere pretence.[1] To tell us that men, who had purchased themselves, or whose fathers had done so, were, at the commencement of a war, expelled from their homesteads and from the lands they had tilled with a promise of reparation if funds should be discovered at the termination of the contest, and to call this compensation, is to mock us. The naked truth is that in the

[1] Chief-Justice Keating addressed his celebrated letter to James on behalf of "many thousands" of the *Purchasers*, the class for which Mr. Lecky says compensation was provided. Keating was of opinion that the compensation was a mere sham. The first sentence of the letter declares that its design is "to prevent the ruin and desolation which a Bill now under consideration in order to be made a law will bring upon them and their families in case your Majesty doth not interpose." Another sentence is, "but the way prescribed by this Bill is to rob the innocent purchasers, creditors, and orphans of their estates, to do it contrary to the public faith, laws of the land, and precept of Holy Writ, etc."

whole black transaction there was not a single bright spot to relieve the darkness of this savage and impolitic Act. No neutral-tinted words can hide from us the enormous proportions of the iniquity. It was the eviction of a people; a universal spoliation, the like of which had not been seen in Europe since the confiscations which followed the Norman Conquest. Tens of thousands of innocent and improving owners,— for all derivative interests (except leases for twenty-one years) went with the fee,—were beggared at a blow, and were thrown homeless and helpless on the world without means and without hope. Such was the selfish greed of the Irish that they paid no regard to a circumstance to which their attention was called, viz. the vast improvements which had been made by the British or Protestant proprietors. James himself tells us "that the improvements had so enhanced the value of most estates as would allow the old proprietors a share of equal income to what their ancestors lost, and yet leave a competency for the purchasers, who might reasonably be allowed the benefit of their own labours."[1] But as the same prince informs us, the Irish "thought of nothing but settling themselves in riches and plenty," and reason and justice were whistled down the wind. If we remember that the Irish Protestants strictly obeyed the law of their country in transferring their allegiance to William, who by the parliamentary grant of the English Crown had become *ipso facto* the rightful sovereign of Ireland, we cannot help considering their fate as hard indeed.

The Act of Repeal not only repealed the Acts of Settlement, but, inasmuch as it went back to the 22d of October 1641, and also included the estates of all those who resided in the parts where James's authority was not recognised and of those who corresponded with them, it confiscated the real property of every Protestant in Ireland, except perhaps [2] that

---

[1] Clarke's *Life*, ii. 358.

[2] I say "perhaps," for if any of these persons were in possession

of the few who attended the Dublin Parliament. But this was not sufficient. It was resolved to confiscate their personal property as well. A short Act was passed for this purpose, entitled an "Act for forfeiting and vesting in His Majesty the goods of absentees." It was enacted that "all goods and chattels, corn in ground, debts by judgment, statutes, bonds, bills, books, or otherwise, and all arrears of rent," of all persons out of the kingdom (infants under the age of seventeen and trustees for non-absent persons only excepted), should be declared forfeited and vested in the king. Immediately after his arrival in Ireland James, as he tells us,[1] had given "orders for seizing the goods of absent Protestants and rebels, making use for that purpose of the most effectual means which the laws of the country permitted, and going even beyond that where the occasion required." If James overstepped the limits of law, it is easy to understand the abuses of authority committed by his subordinates, of whose acts we have many complaints. It is significant of what the treatment of the Protestants was, and of the intention to disregard their rights, that there was no provision in the Act for restoring their personal property to such as should return and prove their innocency.

For the purpose of completely separating Ireland from England, this Parliament passed an Act declaring the independence of the Irish Legislature, and that the English Parliament possessed no authority over it. Thus at last was the dream of the Celtic Irish fulfilled. Roman Catholic ascendency was complete; the land was again in the possession of the natives; and the last link which bound them to England was broken. All this was accomplished, but so also was the ruin of their country.

of estates which had been forfeited for the rebellion of 1641, they came under the provision which revested from the 22d of October 1641 all the original estates in the former proprietors.

[1] *Life of James II*, written by himself; Macpherson's *Original Papers,* i. 192.

If the beggaring and ruin of the Irish Protestants had been the only objects of the Dublin legislators, their aims would have been amply attained by the Act of Repeal, and by that for the forfeiture of the goods and chattels of absentees. But the madmen who surrounded James were not satisfied with Acts directed against property. They resolved to attack the persons of those whom they regarded as their enemies.

Now that Ireland was her own mistress, a feeling which has always been a powerful factor in Irish movements, race-hatred, made its appearance. James had been long aware of the existence of this feeling. In a letter [1] to the king, Lord Clarendon reminds him of a former conversation which took place between them on this matter. "When I had the honour to discourse with your Majesty upon the affairs of this country, you were pleased to say that you looked upon the differences here to be rather between English and Irish than between Catholic and Protestant; which certainly, sir, is a most true notion." So strong was this race-hatred, and so far was it carried at this time, that the Celtic Irish proposed to exclude from their party all Roman Catholics of English descent.[2] Not content with the impoverishment and ruin of the Protestants, and urged on by their antipathy to everything English, the Irish Legislature resolved upon their destruction, and extorted the reluctant consent of James to "a portentous law—a law without a parallel in the history of civilised nations—the great Act of Attainder." By this Act two thousand four hundred and forty-five persons of all ages, sexes, and degrees were proscribed by name; of whom two were archbishops; one, a duke; sixty-three, temporal lords; twenty-two,

---

[1] Letter to the King, 14th March 1686.
[2] "Aber vor ihren Augen bekamen die nativistischen und antienglischen Tendenzen in Irland die oberhand. Ich finde selbst, dass man damals die Katholiken englischer Herkunft auszuschliessen drohte, denn das seien eben die schlimmsten Feinde von Altirland."— RANKE.

ladies; seven, bishops; eighty-five, knights and baronets; eighty-three, clergymen; and two thousand one hundred and eighty-two, esquires, gentlemen, and tradesmen. All these persons—that is the whole Protestant nobility, gentry, and traders of Ireland—were "declared and adjudged traitors convicted and attainted of high treason," and were to suffer, in the words of the Act itself, "such pains of death, penalties, and forfeitures respectively as in cases of high treason are accustomed," unless they, by certain days fixed in the Act, surrendered themselves to such justice as was then administered to Protestants in Dublin.

The manner of inserting names on this record of penalties and death, and the haste with which it was drawn, were equally remarkable. Any member who had a personal quarrel or enmity against another, or desired his estate, or owed him a debt, had only to hand in his name to the clerk at the table, and it was inserted without discussion. No difficulty was made in any case except that of Lord Strafford, and a few words disposed of the objection. As to the haste with which the list was drawn up, we are told that "perhaps no man ever heard of such a crude, imperfect thing, so ill digested and composed, passed in the world for a law. We find the same person brought in under different qualifications. In one place he is expressly allowed till the 1st of October to come in and submit to trial, and yet in another place he is attainted if he do not come in by the 1st of September. Many are attainted by wrong names. Many have their Christian names left out, and many whose names and surnames are both put in are not distinguished by any character whereby they may be known from others of the same name."[1] Owing to this haste many escaped by accident, as did the Fellows and Scholars of Trinity College, and many of the king's adherents were included. The most remarkable of

[1] King.

these were Dodwell, "the most learned man of whom the Jacobite party could boast;"[1] Colonel Keating, who was then actually serving in James's army before Derry; and Lord Mountjoy, who was imprisoned in France, whither he had been sent by Tyrconnel himself.[2]

The savage cruelty of an Act which doomed thousands to the gallows and the quartering-block is abhorrent to human nature, but the chicanery with which it was conceived and carried out was even more detestable. It has been mentioned that days were fixed in the Act before which the attainted persons must surrender themselves. It was known that such a surrender was physically impossible. The 1st of October was the latest date for surrendering. There was an exceedingly strict embargo laid on all vessels in Ireland, so that not a single ship or boat was suffered to pass thence to England before the 1st of November. The embargo was equally strict on the other side, so that it was impossible for the attainted, even if they had notice of the law, to return and surrender themselves. But good care was taken that the sufferers should have no notice until the last day of grace had long[3] expired. The Act took away the power of pardon from the king, unless the pardon was enrolled before the last day of November. To prevent the attainted persons knowing that their names appeared on the list, it was kept carefully concealed. Some Protestant adherents of James were anxious to know whether any of their friends had been proscribed, and tried to obtain a sight of the list. Solicitation and

---

[1] "Who, for the unpardonable crime of having a small estate in Mayo, had been attainted by the Popish Parliament at Dublin."— MACAULAY.

[2] Two columns of this list of doom, one taken from the front and the other from the back of the same page, are given in the Appendix.

[3] Harris and King say four months. "The Act was kept concealed in the custody of the Chancellor. The king, four months afterwards, learned by an accident the force of a law which so much entrenched on his own prerogative."—*Macpherson*, i. 629.

bribery proved vain. Not a single copy got abroad till the time limited for pardon had expired. When James learned that the power of pardoning had been taken from him by the Act, he was indignant, and remonstrated with Nagle, the Attorney-General.[1] This officer had the impertinence to remind the king that he had read the Act before giving his consent to it. The king replied that he had depended upon his Attorney-General for drawing the Act, and that if Nagle had drawn it so that there was no room for pardoning, he had been false to his sovereign, and had betrayed him. When the same Nagle,[2] as Speaker of the Commons, presented this Bill of Attainder to James for his consent, he was not ashamed to say that many were attainted upon such evidence as fully satisfied the House, and the rest were attainted "upon common fame." Nagle was a Roman Catholic lawyer of repute, yet, on such a solemn occasion, he did not hesitate to say that common fame or report was sufficient evidence to deprive thousands of his fellow-citizens of their lives and fortunes.

All impartial readers of history are appalled by the magnitude of this legislative scheme of judicial murder. The Irish Roman Catholic writers palliate, or, what is more shameful, conceal it. They cannot see that, in so doing, they make themselves participators in the crime of their fathers, and that, in declining to award historical justice to the misdeeds of their ancestors, they unconsciously prove the hereditary transmission of political incapacity to their race. The rule of duty that recognition of the sin, acknowledgment of the error is the first step to repentance, is as true in public as in

---

[1] James complains in his Memoirs that he was obliged to give up his prerogative of pardon in this Act.—Clarke's *Life*, ii. 361.

[2] Nagle was the first man who ventured openly to propose the repeal of the Acts of Settlement. In his Coventry letter of 26th October 1686 he advocated their repeal, chiefly on the ground that they weakened the Roman Catholic interest in Ireland.

private life. But this rule is unknown, or, if known, is not practised, by these authors and apologists. O'Connor calls the Act of Attainder a state engine. Plowden says, it contains not one word relating to religious distinction, as if an open reference to such a motive of this kind would be allowed to appear at such a crisis. Curry, M'Geoghegan, and Cusack are silent respecting it. M'Gee's expressions are, " an Act of Attainder against persons in arms against the sovereign whose estates lay in Ireland was adopted." Haverty dismisses it as if it referred merely to property. His words are: " As to the Act of Attainder, passed on the same occasion, its results, so far as the question of property was concerned, would have been nearly identical with those of the Act of Settlement, the persons who would be affected by both being nearly the same." It would be difficult to compose sentences more misleading than those of these two latter authors.

Some of these writers have excused the Act of Attainder on the ground that no blood was actually shed under its authority. As well might the assassin who laid a spring-gun with the object of murder excuse himself on the ground that his intended victim had returned by another path. Fortunately for those threatened by the Act, they were beyond the reach of their vindictive enemies. An early flight had saved them. We can only judge of the intentions of men by their acts. If the Irish Legislature did not desire blood, why were the pains and penalties of death inserted in this enactment, when forfeiture of property only would have effected the ruin of their adversaries? And why was the Act concealed till the last day of grace had expired? Why, too, was the power of pardon withdrawn from the king? As long as these questions remain unanswered, there is but one conclusion to which reasonable men can come. And that conclusion is, that if the refugees had returned, and the English deliverer had not appeared, there would have been another bloody page added to the history of this country.

Mr. Lecky, in his remarks on this infamous Act of Attainder, has made the extraordinary statement that a Bill of Attainder "precisely similar" to that of the Irish Parliament was brought forward in the English Commons and was passed in that House. This is an astounding assertion. It takes away our breath to hear that in the seventeenth century a barbarous and bloody Bill of general proscription was introduced and passed in a civilised assembly such as the Commons of England. Very little is known of this English Bill, as the references to it in the Journals of the House are short and compendious, but fortunately the clause which confiscates the estates of those attainted by it survives, and enables us to arrive at the number affected.[1] They are exactly eighteen in number, all persons well known to the English Parliament. What "precise similarity" can exist between an Act which proscribed the whole nobility, gentry, and trading community of a country, whose names and whose guilt or innocence could not possibly have been known to the Parliament which doomed them, and a bill which attainted eighteen influential adherents of James, the majority of whom had fled from England with him, I am unable to see. Mr. Lecky actually taunts Macaulay with not having disclosed this English Bill.

By an Act of this Parliament the payment of tithes by Roman Catholics to the Protestant clergy was abolished. For three years before the passing of the Act hardly any tithes had been recovered by the Protestant clergy. The priests had begun, even so early as 1685, to declare that the tithes belonged to them, and they had forbidden the people to pay them as the law required.[2] They said openly that the king, who was anxious to protect the Protestants, had no power to interfere

---

[1] *Journals of the House of Commons*, x. 269.
[2] Lord Clarendon to the King, 14th August 1686.

with the property of the Church. The Dublin Parliament now confirmed this violation of the law. To reduce the endowments of the Protestant Church, says Macaulay, "without prejudice to existing interests, would have been a reform worthy of a good prince and of a good Parliament. But no such reform would satisfy the vindictive bigots who sate at the King's Inns. By one sweeping Act the greater part of the tithe was transferred from the Protestant to the Roman Catholic clergy; and the existing incumbents were left, without one farthing of compensation, to die of hunger."

There was an appearance of justice attending the Act for the transference of the tithes to the Roman Catholic priesthood, notwithstanding that vested interests were cruelly and ruthlessly passed over. Nothing can be said in favour of another law which accompanied that for the abolition of tithes. At this time there was hardly a Roman Catholic householder in the corporate towns and cities. These corporate towns, with the exception of Dublin, Cork, Limerick, Galway, and Waterford, had been built at the expense and charges of the Protestant settlers. In these towns a small rate or tax had been imposed on houses by Act of Parliament,[1] and this tax was payable to the Protestant clergymen who ministered there. This was, therefore, a matter exclusively between the Protestants and their own clergy. James desired sincerely to protect the Protestant clergy of Ireland, for they had espoused his interest most cordially when he was Duke of York, and his right to the succession questioned. But the Irish legislators were resolved to make the country Roman Catholic, and they passed an Act abolishing these payments for the maintenance of the Protestant ministers in towns. By these two Acts all the endowments of the Protestant Church, and all the provision made for the maintenance of her clergy, were at one blow swept away. Her ministers were left to

---

[1] 17 and 18 Charles II, c. 7.

the charity of their flocks, or death by starvation. It excites a smile when we read that these two Acts were accompanied by a third in favour of liberty of conscience. It was a strange conjunction, and worthy of this Parliament—liberty of conscience and the starvation of ministers of religion. We must not, however, forget that the Act for liberty of conscience was the work of James, and that the other two proceeded from fanatics and bigots.

In the meantime the sins of the Executive fully equalled the mad criminality of the Legislature. I do not here speak of the debasement of the coinage and the innumerable oppressions committed under and by means of it;[1] the second and third disarming of the Protestants; the press for horses; the quarterings of soldiers; and the extortion and robberies committed by them.[2] These things the Roman Catholic apologists have excused, on the ground that a state of war prevailed, and that every Protestant was a rebel at heart. I shall not even mention the general seizure of Protestant schools throughout the country, and the attack on Trinity College. But there were other proceedings, to justify which no attempt has ever been made, and respecting which a judicious silence

---

[1] "A mortgage for a thousand pounds was cleared off by a bag of counters made out of old kettles. The creditors, who complained to the Court of Chancery, were told by Fitton to take their money and be gone. But of all classes the tradesmen of Dublin, who were generally Protestants, were the greatest losers. Any man who belonged to the caste now dominant might walk into a shop, lay on the counter a bit of brass worth threepence, and carry off goods to the value of half a guinea."—MACAULAY.

[2] "The misery of this town is very great, some being little better than dragooned by the quartering of soldiers; some have ten, some twelve, some twenty or thirty, quartered on them; and yet I cannot find that, besides what came in to-day, there were above three thousand and odd men in town. But the reason is plain: each man has many quarters, and some captains make thirty or forty shillings a week by them. They come in by twelve, one, or two of the clock by night to demand quarters, and turn people out of their beds, beat, wound, and sometimes rob them."—*Letter from Dublin*, 12th June 1689.

has been observed. While the Irish Legislature was overturning the established order of things, a persecution of the Protestants was raging, with the connivance of the Government, through the three provinces which owned James's authority. These provinces were quiet, and their Protestant inhabitants made a merit of their obedience. Yet they were obliged to witness what the king himself called the general desolation of the land, and to suffer, in James's words, " many robberies, oppressions, and outrages, committed through all parts of the kingdom to the utter ruin thereof, and to the great scandal of the Government, as well as of Christianity." There was a complete relaxation of all civil and military authority [1] through these provinces, though untouched by war. The judges neglected their duties; the justices of the peace acted illegally and in favour of malefactors, and the officers and soldiers of the army contributed to the general anarchy.[2] All peasantries outrun the wishes of their Government when they suppose those wishes are favourable to them. The hints of further rapine given in the Acts of Attainder and Repeal of the Settlement were greedily received and speedily acted on by that of Ireland.[3] The Protestants were scattered, unarmed and defenceless, among a hostile and barbarous population, and the Government of Tyrconnel connived at their ruin. When that is said, all is said. The pathetic consists in details, and the heart cannot take in more than one picture

---

[1] Instructions of James to the Commissioners of Oyer and Terminer. They are given in the appendix to King.

[2] "Jamais troupes n'ont marché comme font celles-cy; ils vont comme des bandits, et pillent tout ce qu'ils trouvent en chemin."—D'AVAUX.

[3] "The miserable usage in the country is unspeakable, and every day like to be worse and worse; many allege that the rapparees have secret orders to fall anew on the Protestants that have anything left; the ground of this may be their pretending such an order, for they commonly pretend an order for any mischief they have a mind to."—*Letter from Dublin*, 1689.

of distress at the same time. The imagination cannot conceive, language is inadequate to describe, the sum-total of individual suffering comprised in the ruin of a whole community.

The accounts of the state of the country do not rest on Protestant testimony alone. During the winter of 1689 James issued, through his principal Secretary of State,[1] instructions to the judges, in which he accused them of "having strangely neglected the execution of their commissions," and stated that this neglect was "the chiefest cause of the general desolation of the country." These instructions are too long to be given in full; but as they are strictly contemporaneous, and afford official information of the state of Ireland, I shall quote two paragraphs : "Let the present general cries of the people for justice, and the present general oppression under which the country groans, move you to have compassion of it, and to raise in you such a public spirit as may save it from this inundation of miseries that breaks in upon it by a neglect of His Majesty's orders, and by a general relaxation of all civil and military laws. Consider that our enemies, leaving us to ourselves, as they do, conclude we shall prove greater enemies to one another than they can be to us, and that we will destroy the country and enslave ourselves more than they are able to do. What inhumanities are daily committed against one another gives but too much ground to the truth of what our enemies conclude of us."

But James's endeavours to reduce the general anarchy, and to restore some degree of law and order, were fruitless. His authority was neglected, and in every step he took he was thwarted and disobeyed by the Irish faction which had him in their power. His unwillingness to consent to the

[1] White, an Irish Catholic, created Marquis d'Albaville by the King of Spain.

Acts of Attainder and Repeal of the Settlement, his struggles to protect his Protestant subjects, and his attempts to secure the administration of justice and the punishment of malefactors, had made him thoroughly unpopular. There was already gathering about him that hatred which has attended his memory in this country, and has attached to his name in Irish a filthy and disgusting word. To the natives James was a foreigner and an Englishman. To one who had lived among civilised men the Irish schemes of extirpation and revenge were hateful and abhorrent.[1]

It has been denied that the churches of the Protestants were seized by the Roman Catholics. Nothing can be more true than that this was done, especially those which had been built on consecrated ground where the chapels of abbeys formerly stood.[2] It is proved beyond all doubt by the petitions of the Protestants, and by James's proclamation,[3] declaring that the seizure of churches was a violation of his Act for liberty of conscience. Archbishop King asserts that nine churches out of ten were taken possession of throughout the country, twenty-six alone in the diocese of Dublin. Leslie denies that a single church, except Christ Church, and that only because it was reputed the king's chapel, was taken by the order or connivance of the king. The assertion and qualified denial are both true. James, we know, was desirous to protect the Protestant clergy, and thus

[1] "But, above all, some of them moving to him for leave to cut off the Protestants, which he returned with indignation and amazement, saying, 'What, gentlemen, are you for another forty-one?'—which so galled them that they ever after looked upon him with a jealous eye, and thought him, though a Roman Catholic, too much an Englishman to carry on their business."—LESLIE.

[2] *A Short View of the Methods made use of in Ireland for the Subversion*, etc., 1689.

[3] "The king published soon after a proclamation for surrendering all the Protestant churches which had been seized upon by the Catholics, and took great care to have all grievances of that nature redressed."—Clarke's *James II.*

to disprove the allegations of his enemies that his liberty of conscience was but a mask assumed for an occasion. But we must draw a distinction between James and the Irish ministers who surrounded him. The latter connived at the claims of the Roman Catholic priesthood and the excesses of an excited population. When the king gave a positive order that the church at Wexford should be restored to the Protestants, the order was eluded or disobeyed by his ministers. Tyrconnel's Government even proceeded so far as to forbid, contrary to the Act for liberty of conscience, the Protestants to assemble in churches or elsewhere on pain of death.[1] Yet this was the Act upon which James rested his hopes of regaining his English throne and conciliating his English subjects.

Leslie, upon whose statements the Irish writers rely, insists strongly upon this distinction between the king and his Irish ministers.[2] He says: "Before I enter upon this disquisition I desire to obviate one objection which I know will be made. As if I were about wholly to vindicate all that Lord Tyrconnel and other of King James's ministers have done in Ireland, especially before this revolution began, and which most of anything brought it on. No; I am far from it. I am sensible that their carriage in many particulars gave greater occasion to King James's enemies than all the other maladministrations which were charged against his Government." And in another place he repeats the statement: "I am very sensible of the many ill steps which were

---

[1] Dalrymple.
[2] Leslie's authority is deservedly high. He was a man of great logical acuteness and of the purest life. He was the son of that bishop who valiantly defended his palace at Raphoe against the parliamentary forces. Leslie conscientiously refused to take the oaths to William and Mary, and was in consequence deprived of his church preferments. He followed James to France, and did not return to Ireland till 1721, where he died in the following year at his house in Glaslough in the county of Monaghan.

made in King James's Government, and, above all, of the mischievous consequences of Lord Tyrconnel's administration, which the most of any one thing brought on the misfortunes of his master."

Such is the story, told in plain unvarnished language, of the Irish Parliament of James II. Twice within forty years had the Irish Roman Catholics attempted to break away from Great Britain, and to establish an independent kingdom under the protection of a Foreign Power. Both attempts, that of 1641 and that of 1688, were undertaken while the attention of Great Britain was turned away from Ireland and occupied with her own domestic disputes with her sovereign. In the first attempt the Irish had possession of the country for eight years, from 1641 to the landing of Cromwell in 1649. The sun never looked down upon such a scene as Ireland exhibited during this period. Violence, pillage, and rapine were universal, and prevailed in every corner of the island, while at the same time rabid animosities divided the several parties which had sprung up from each other, and forbade their union. Ireland was a land of Ishmaels, where every man's hand was directed against his brother. The results of the internecine and multifarious contests may be told in words, but the imagination cannot even attempt to picture to itself the horrors of the situation in which the country stood at the end of the rebellion. Ireland had become a desert in which wolves had taken the place of men. More than six hundred thousand of its inhabitants had perished in the war,[1] or by the famine and pestilence which accompanied it.

In 1688 the Irish again obtained a momentary possession of the country, and the same results which had attended the former followed the second attempt. But these results were

[1] Petty says 616,000.

of shorter duration in 1688, owing to the speedier interference of Great Britain.¹ In their short ascendency of four years, the Irish did nothing but pillage, confiscate, and attaint. During this limited period they slaughtered hundreds of thousands of cattle and sheep, and once more turned Ireland into a desert. Besides the destruction of 100,000 lives, the waste committed by the Irish from 1686 to 1690 was so great that it was estimated that it would take twenty years of steady industry to replace the loss which the country had undergone.

If the rebels of 1641, or if the crew of Irish and French adventurers who were in temporary possession of the country in 1688 had succeeded in their efforts, they would have destroyed the British colony in Ireland, and its destruction would have been a loss to the civilised world. For that colony, like the nation from the bosom of which it sprang, has also been the *alma virum mater;* the nursing mother of heroes, statesmen, administrators, poets, and orators. It is remarkable what a long list of eminent men this small off-shoot of the Anglo-Saxon race has contributed to the roll of British worthies. Their names are known and their voices are heard wherever the English language is spoken. I need only mention some of the names on this register of honour; many more will occur to the memory of every reader— Boyle, Burke, Berkeley, Canning, Castlereagh, Clare, Usher, Wellington, Wellesley, the two Lawrences, Sterne, Swift, Edgeworth, Grattan, Plunket, Goldsmith, Steele, Napier.

---

[1] Mr. Gladstone must have had in view such interpositions of Great Britain as those of 1641, 1688, and 1798, when he delivered the following admirable words: "My firm belief is that the influence of Great Britain in every Irish difficulty is not a domineering and tyrannising but a softening and mitigating influence, and that were Ireland detached from her political connection with this country, and left to her own unaided agencies, it might be that the strife of parties would then burst forth in a form calculated to strike horror through the land."—Hansard's *Parliamentary Debates,* clxxxi. 721.

Nor has the seed failed or the race degenerated. Their successors are worthy of the inheritance of high endeavour which has been handed down to them.

The quick-witted Irish Celt has taken advantage of a generic word, "Irish," and has claimed these eminent citizens as his kinsmen and as witnesses of the capacity of his race. But the claim is unfounded and cannot be maintained. The distinguished men of whom I have been speaking were the products of a different civilisation, and of a widely different culture from that of the Irish Celt. They were British to the backbone, reared on British pap, and nourished on the living traditions of the British peoples. *They* had not been taught that history, as narrated by Protestant writers, was a fable; that the Reformation was a crime, or at the best a fatal step backwards; that our martyrs were rebels against divine authority; and that our great Elizabeth was a bastard and a wanton. Nor had they been fed on the audacious falsehoods and half-truths which misrepresent the conduct of Great Britain to Ireland, and nourish hatred and disaffection to her government and institutions.[1] Sharers in

---

[1] Mr. Gladstone has described in vigorous language the teaching which has been addressed to the Irish Celts: "What that literature is is well known. It is well known how it *teaches* and *preaches* in every form, with an amount of boldness and audacity varying from week to week and from month to month, *hatred of the institutions and government of the United Kingdom.* It is known how that weekly literature *poisons the minds of the people in Ireland* who read it *against all law* and *against the constitution* of their country. It is known how it *inflames the passions* of the people by rhetorical descriptions of the *wrongs of other days.* It is known how it makes it impossible for those who read that literature, and read none other, to know the truth with respect to public affairs and the real conduct and intentions of the Government of the country. It is well known how constantly —sometimes openly and undisguisedly, sometimes under some disguise more or less thin—it points, not to any constitutional means for the redress of what may be deemed grievances, *not to any action within the law and constitution, but to violence and civil war.*"—*Hansard,* cc. 100, 17th March 1870.

the labours which contributed to the making of the common country, they loved to consider themselves as fellow-workmen in building up a renowned empire. No thought of disunion, no forgetfulness of common aims, ever palsied their arms or drove them to stand apart in sullen discontent. It would have been an irreparable loss, not only to the United Realm but to the world, if, in the religious convulsions of Ireland, which were only chapters in the general religious strife of Europe, the community which produced these men had been crushed out of existence, or its higher civilisation subordinated to a lower.

CHAPTER II

THE ALLEGED VIOLATION OF THE TREATY
OF LIMERICK

SECTION I

THE SECOND SIEGE AND TREATY OF LIMERICK [1]

AFTER the well-contested battle of Aughrim, on the 12th of July 1691, the defeated Irish army divided, one branch taking its way to Galway, the other to Limerick. The English army marched first to Galway, whither some regiments of Irish, thinned by the slaughter at Aughrim and utterly demoralised, had repaired under the command of D'Usson and Lord Dillon. On the 21st of July Galway surrendered on terms; the garrison was permitted to retire to Limerick, a full amnesty for past offences was granted, and it was agreed that the names of the Roman Catholic clergy should be given in to the English general, and that they, as well as the laity of the place, should be allowed the private exercise of their religion without being prosecuted on any penal laws for the same.[2]

From Galway Ginkell and the English army advanced slowly to Limerick and appeared before that town on the 26th of August, on which day the second siege commenced.[3]

---

[1] In 1788 Dr. Arthur Browne, fellow of Trinity College and representative in the Irish Parliament for the University of Dublin, published a pamphlet entitled, *A Brief Review of the question whether the Articles of Limerick have been violated?* I have made use of this publication. The author does not mention the proposals first made by the garrison, which, in my opinion, give the key to the whole matter.

[2] Story, *Continuation*, p. 166.

[3] *Ib.* and *Diary of the Siege of Limerick*, Dublin, 1692. The 26th of August is the 5th of September as we count now.

Two successful engagements were fought by Ginkell's troops under the walls, the second of which, that at Thomond bridge, wrought such an effect that a parley was beaten by the besieged on the next day, the 23d of September. Less than a month's resistance had tamed the courage or exhausted the patience of the Irish leaders. They were eager to capitulate, Sarsfield the most eager of them all. A gallant soldier, Colonel Kelly, an actor in and a describer of these scenes, informs us, that what "raised the admiration of all people and begat an astonishment which seemed universal over all Ireland, was the sudden unexpected prodigious change of Sarsfield, who appeared now the most active of all the commanders to forward the treaty, and took most pains to persuade the tribunes and centurions to a compliance. . . . Sarsfield, in whom the Irish nation reposed their greatest confidence, and who, as they all believed, would be the last man to hearken to a treaty, was now the most earnest to press it on."[1] Negotiations were opened by the Irish, and hostages were exchanged with a view to a further and permanent treaty. On the 27th of September the garrison sent a paper to Ginkell containing the terms on which they were willing to surrender. These terms proposed by the Irish were seven in number :—

"1. That their Majesties will by an Act of indemnity pardon all past crimes and offences whatsoever.

"2. To restore all Irish Catholics to the estates of which they were seized or possessed before the late revolution.

"3. To allow a free liberty of worship, and one priest to each parish, as well in towns and cities as in the country.

"4. Irish Catholics to be capable of bearing employments, military and civil, and to exercise professions, trades, callings, of what nature soever.

[1] *Macariæ Excidium*, published by the Irish Archæological Society.

"5. The Irish army to be kept on foot, paid, etc., as the rest of their Majesties' forces, in case they be willing to serve their Majesties against France or any other enemy.

"6. The Irish Catholics to be allowed to live in towns corporate and cities, to be members of corporations, to exercise all sorts and manners of trade, and to be equal with their fellow Protestant subjects in all privileges, advantages, and immunities accruing in or by the said corporations.

"7. An Act of Parliament to be passed for ratifying and confirming the said conditions."[1]

When these proposals of the Irish were submitted to Ginkell, they were at once rejected.[2] That general said that "though he was in a manner a stranger to the laws of England, yet he understood that those things they insisted upon were so far contradictory to them and dishonourable to himself that he would not grant any such terms."[3] Ginkell immediately ordered an additional battery to be thrown up for mortars and guns. The rejection of their terms cast a duty upon the Irish leaders of which they were incapable, and which they certainly did not perform. They were even unconscious of it, for Ginkell was interrupted in his preparations by another message from the garrison asking him to let them know what terms he was ready to offer. In answer to this message Ginkell sent them twelve articles much the same as those which were afterwards agreed on,[4] and declared that he would allow of no others. These articles were accepted by the Irish on the 28th of September, and it was arranged that there should be a cessation of arms until the arrival of the Lords Justices from Dublin.

The original proposals of the garrison deserve our most careful attention, for they and the rejection of them by

---

[1] Story, *Cont.* p. 230.
[2] "The general returned them with disdain."—*Diary of the Siege.*
[3] Story, *Cont.* p. 230.   [4] *Ib.* p. 231.

Ginkell throw a flood of light upon the subsequent treaty, and upon what the Irish understood they were to get by that treaty. The Irish had demanded that they should enjoy freedom of worship; that it should be declared that they were capable of civil and military employment; that they should not be debarred from exercising any trades or professions; that they should be privileged to become members of corporations; and that they should be allowed to dwell in corporate towns and cities. These demands were all at once repudiated by Ginkell as being "contradictory" to the laws. Yet, on the very next morning, the Irish leaders, knowing that these demands had been rejected as totally inadmissible, sent commissioners to the English camp, who then and there accepted the only terms which Ginkell considered himself authorised to offer. It is therefore evident that the Irish, when they accepted the articles which Ginkell conceded, and which were afterwards drawn out into the treaty of Limerick, were well aware—(1) that freedom for their worship would not be granted; (2) that no Irish Roman Catholic was to be capable of civil or military employ; (3) that Irish Catholics would not be allowed to exercise every trade and profession; (4) that they were not to be members of corporations; and (5) that they were not to be permitted to dwell in corporate towns or cities. The Irish, knowing that their own conditions had been rejected as illegal, were content to accept and sign others. However the final treaty might be drawn, it is certain that not one of the rejected terms was expected by either party to be included in it. Ginkell had repudiated the whole body of them as being contradictory to the laws; the Irish leaders, by continuing the negotiations after their demands had been rejected, waived those which they had formerly made. If written documents and acts done at a supreme crisis have any meaning, it is beyond doubt that the English general repudiated each and every claim of the Irish, and that the Irish leaders after such repudiation agreed to surrender Limerick upon other and lower terms, which they knew did not include a single demand put forward previously by them on behalf of the Irish Roman Catholics.

Readers will observe the seventh demand of the Irish, that an Act of Parliament should be passed to confirm what they asked for. It was not in the power of the king, as the executive, to grant terms which would have altered the whole law of the land and abolished all the restrictions which were imposed on the Roman Catholics. That could be effected by the Legislature alone. That this was well understood by the Irish is shown by this demand.

On the 1st of October the Lords Justices, Coningsby and Porter, arrived in the camp, and on the 3d what is commonly called the Treaty of Limerick was signed.[1] The use of the singular number is misleading, for there were in fact two treaties, the one civil, containing thirteen articles, and the other military, containing twenty-nine. The military treaty was subscribed by the generals on both sides only; the civil treaty was signed by Ginkell and also by the Lords Justices on behalf of the king.

With the military treaty we have comparatively little to do. It was absolute and subject to no subsequent revision. Its terms contained nothing which did not lie within the power of the executive to grant, nor was it necessary that they, unlike those of the civil treaty, should be submitted to Parliament for its confirmation and approval. By its articles it was agreed that such Irish and French officers and soldiers as should declare their wish to go to France should be conveyed thither, and should in the meantime remain under the command of their own superiors; that Ginkell should furnish a sufficiency of vessels to carry the troops to France; and

[1] The treaty is given in the Appendix.

that there should be a cessation of arms on land and at sea with respect to the ships designed for the transportation of the army until they should return to their respective harbours. The military treaty was strictly complied with, and all its terms were honourably carried out. Not only were the regular Irish and French troops duly conveyed, but even the rapparees and partisans were furnished with the means of transport. Many of the Irish soldiers afterwards refused to proceed to France, but this they did in consequence of letters and reports received from those who had been already conveyed there as to the manner in which the first arrivals had been treated in France. No opposition was offered to the departure of any. We know from Story that the Irish troops on their march to embark at Cork deserted in dozens; and on the 8th of December three entire regiments, Colonel Macdermot's, Colonel Brian O'Neill's, and Colonel Felix O'Neill's, part of the army designed for France, refused to go, broke up, and returned to their homes.[1] That the agreement to furnish a sufficiency of transports was also loyally observed, we have the evidence of Sarsfield himself, who, in December, released the English general from providing any further shipping. "Whereas," such is the wording of the release, "by the articles of Limerick, Lieutenant-General Ginkell, commander-in-chief of the English army, did engage himself to furnish ten thousand ton of shipping for the transporting of such of the Irish forces to France as were willing to go thither; and to facilitate their passage, to add four thousand ton more, in case the French fleet did not come to this kingdom to take off part of these forces; and whereas the French fleet has been upon the coast and carried away some of the said forces, and the Lieutenant-General has provided ships for as many of the rest as are willing to go as aforesaid, I do hereby declare that the said Lieutenant-General is released

[1] Story, *Cont.* p. 291.

from any obligation he lay under from the said articles to provide vessels for that purpose, and do quit and renounce all further claim and pretension on this account."[1]

The importance to the Irish leaders of the military treaty and of the transport of the Irish troops to France has been minimised or kept out of sight. It is hard to understand how a garrison, well furnished with arms and fully provisioned,[2] surrendered to an army which did not exceed it in numbers; and that too at a time when everything was in favour of a prolonged defence. The only effectual way of reducing the town was to invest it on all sides. To do this, it would have been necessary to divide the English army, and a division of the forces would have given the predominance to the enemy.[3] The season was far advanced, the winter was near and the rains had set in. The whole plain about the city might shortly become a lake of stagnant water. It would then be necessary to remove the English army to a healthier and drier spot than could be found on the banks of the Shannon. If so, the siege would have to be turned into a blockade, as, indeed, had lately been urged in a council of war on the 17th September in the English camp. The city

[1] Story, *Cont.* p. 292.

[2] "The garrison was well supplied with provisions, they were provided with all means of defence."—Macpherson, *History of Great Britain*, i. 695. "The garrison was healthy, well supplied, and in numbers equal to their assailants."—*Leland*, iii. 611.

[3] "It was dangerous for the besiegers to continue in their present station on the approach of winter, and hazardous to divide an army sufficient only for assailing the town on one side; and yet the only effectual way of reducing it was to invest it on all sides, by cutting off the garrison from all intercourse with the county of Clare." "The besieging army had made no impression on the principal part of the city; it was inferior in numbers to that of the garrison; winter was fast approaching, and at the very moment French succours were on the coast."—Parnell's *Historical Apology for the Irish Catholics*. The apologist does not see that in recording these facts he is recording the disgrace of the Irish leaders who prematurely surrendered the city. When the English took possession of the town, Story found all the works "exceeding strong."—*Cont.* p. 256.

would then have been safe till the spring, and long before the spring the promised succours from France, which were known to be on their way, would have arrived. The contest could then have been carried on till the condition was insisted on that a Parliament should be called and a real improvement effected in the position of the Roman Catholics under the sanction of the Legislature. Had this been done, had the Irish leaders conducted an obstinate defence, instead of a mere show of defence, they might have done something more for their Roman Catholic brethren than leave behind them their signatures to an illusory document. They might have effected something for an unfortunate people whom they themselves had called to arms, and whom they were now preparing to desert in their utmost need.

It was indeed a mystery at the time, as Colonel Kelly tells us, why the Irish leaders were so eager to surrender, "a mystery which requires some further time to unriddle." So anxious were these gentlemen to conclude the capitulation, that they signed the articles without the clause, afterwards known as the disputed clause, which they subsequently asked Ginkell to insert; nor did they make any conditions for the restoration of the estates of prisoners; or for the orphans of those who had been slain in the service of him whom they regarded as their king.[1] But what was most shameful of all, they made no efforts, as we shall see, after their first proposals, to secure liberty for the Roman Catholic worship or a single condition for their bishops and clergy. Well might a brave and single-minded soldier exclaim, "That the most zealous Roman Catholics of the universe should conclude a peace with the sworn enemy of the true worship without conditions for their sacred bishops or obtaining security for their free exercise of the divine ceremonies, is a mystery that surpasses the weak capacity of man to comprehend."[2]

[1] *Macariæ Excidium.*   [2] *Ib.*

The Duke of Berwick, who had been so lately among these leaders and had served with them, furnishes us with the key to the mystery. The Irish commanders were eager to be gone to fresh fields and pastures new, where they might acquire military rank and consequence. "They" [the Irish commissioners], says the Duke, "were much to blame in neglecting to include in the agreement all the Irish in general; for the generals of the enemy would have consented to everything for the sake of putting an end to the war; but the incapacity of the deputies who were entrusted by the garrison to conduct the capitulation, and perhaps the fear that this proposition might be an obstacle to the transportation of the troops, which some persons for views of private interest were particularly desirous of, might be the reason why it was not even mentioned."[1] It was of the utmost importance to the Irish commanders to carry with them to their new country a large and effective body of soldiers. Upon their doing so depended their future rank and position. France possessed a numerous and gallant army of her own, proud of its achievements, and jealous of the order of promotion. It was not likely that solitary exiles unaccompanied by followers would obtain high rank in such an army. But if those exiles could bring with them a numerous and efficient body of troops, capable of forming an army in itself, all this would be changed and their position and prospects would be assured. Hence it is that out of the twenty-nine articles of the military treaty, and the thirteen of the civil treaty, or forty-two in all, one short and illusory paragraph only is devoted to the claims of the general body of the Roman Catholics—a clause too which makes no attempt to improve their condition, but leaves them to suffer in the future as they had suffered in the past. The Irish Roman Catholics have always felt, and felt with justice, that there was something

[1] *Mémoires du Maréchal de Berwick*, i. 102.

wrong, some one to blame, in the matter of the Treaty of Limerick. Misled by their hatred of England and by the audacious assertions of their writers, they have placed the blame on the wrong shoulders. They have not perceived that the blame attached, not to King William or to the Irish Parliament, but to their own trusted but incompetent and fainthearted leaders.

We now come to the civil treaty, which differed from the military convention in one essential point. It was conditional on the approbation and confirmation of the Irish Parliament, to the ratification of which it was made expressly subject. The military convention related to matters which were to be immediately carried into effect, and which lay within the power of the king to grant or refuse. The civil treaty referred to the *status* of the general body of the Roman Catholics of Ireland, and to things which were beyond the power of the Executive and required the sanction of the Legislature. From the very nature of the matters treated of in it, even if there had not been a special stipulation to that effect, the civil articles must have been laid before the Parliament for its confirmation. There are thirteen articles in the civil treaty, all of which, except one, relate to individuals or classes of persons then in existence. It is evident that no privileges can be claimed for a national body under terms which refer to particular times or specified individuals. The first article is the only one which relates to the general body of the Irish Roman Catholics, and it and the twelfth make the whole treaty conditional on its ratification by Parliament.

"1. The Roman Catholics of this kingdom shall enjoy such privileges in the exercise of their religion as are consistent with the laws of Ireland, or as they did enjoy in the reign of King Charles the Second; and their Majesties, as soon as their affairs will permit them to summon a Parliament in this kingdom, will endeavour to procure the said Roman

Catholics such further security in that particular as may preserve them from any disturbance upon the account of the said religion."

"12. Lastly, the Lords Justices and General do undertake that their Majesties will ratify these articles within the space of eight months or sooner, and will use their utmost endeavours that the same shall be ratified and confirmed in Parliament."

It might be thought on reading the first clause that the Roman Catholics of Ireland had enjoyed privileges in the reign of Charles II which this treaty endeavoured to revive, and that they looked back fondly on their social position in that reign. As a matter of fact, no change whatever had been made in their state since that reign. They were, when the treaty was negotiated, exactly in the same position which they had occupied in the reign of Charles. No alteration had taken place except that during their short ascendency under James all law had been violated, and the Constitution overturned. What takes place in the treaty is in effect this: "We are to remain then," say the Irish commissioners, "in the same state and subject to all the restrictions and disabilities we now labour under." "Yes," reply the Lords Justices; "the general has already refused to grant the proposals made by you, as contradictory to the law. To change that law requires the interposition of the Legislature; all we can offer is a promise that the king will endeavour to obtain a mitigation of your lot from that Legislature." The Irish leaders, with arms in their hands, with a large and disciplined force at their back which equalled in number the English army, and with French aid on its way,[1] were content to yield up their last citadel in return for a promise the fulfilment of which they knew did not depend on the king, but upon the

---

[1] The French succours arrived within three days after the treaty was signed.

will of a Parliament which was not in existence, and which had not been summoned for more than a quarter of a century.

That this is the meaning of the only clause in favour of the Roman Catholics is evident when we remember that that body was then precisely in the same position in which it had been in the reign of Charles II. This will appear more clearly if the condition of the Roman Catholics at that time be fully set out. The following was the position of that body in the last year of Charles II:—

1. It was a criminal offence, punishable the second time with imprisonment for life, for a Roman Catholic ecclesiastic to say mass.[1]

2. It was a criminal offence, punishable the third time with imprisonment for life, for any Roman Catholic to hear mass.[2]

3. Every Roman Catholic was bound, under a pecuniary penalty, to attend a Protestant church.[3]

4. No Roman Catholic priest could remain in Ireland without taking the oath of supremacy and renouncing the authority of the Pope in civil matters.[4]

5. No Roman Catholic priest could enter the kingdom without taking the same oath, and renouncing the same authority.[5]

6. Every Roman Catholic, knowing that a priest had not taken the oath of supremacy, was bound to inform against him under penalties of fine and imprisonment.[6]

7. No Roman Catholic could act as a schoolmaster, or even as a private tutor, without taking the oath of supremacy and renouncing the authority of the Pope.[7]

---

[1] 2 Eliz. c. 2, § 2.
[2] This was decided on the word "maintain" in the third section of the 2 Eliz.   [3] 2 Eliz. c. 2, § 3.
[4] 27 Eliz. c. 2, an English Act extending to all Her Majesty's dominions.
[5] *Ib.*   [6] *Ib.*   [7] 17 and 18 Chas. II, c. 6, § 6.

8. No Roman Catholic could send his children abroad to be educated without the special license of the Privy Council,[1] and Protestant guardians might be appointed to Roman Catholic wards.[2]

9. No Roman Catholic could be a justice of the peace, mayor, recorder, alderman, magistrate, or burgess of any corporation.[3]

10. No Roman Catholic could purchase or take a lease of a house within any corporate town without the license of the Lord Lieutenant and Privy Council.[4]

11. By an order of the Parliament in the reign of Charles II, no Roman Catholic could sit as a member without taking the oath of supremacy and renouncing the authority of the Pope.[5]

In addition to these restrictions, proclamations and prohibitious forbidding the exercise of the Roman Catholic religion were occasionally issued in the reign of Charles II. Thus in this reign a proclamation was issued ordering all Roman Catholic artisans and shopkeepers to depart from Kilkenny and the other large towns.[6] In 1666 the Lord Lieutenant banished a large part of the Catholic clergy out of the kingdom, so that there were only three bishops remaining in the country.[7] And in 1679 a proclamation was issued that Roman Catholic ecclesiastics should depart from the kingdom, and that their seminaries and convents should be suppressed.[8]

Such was the strictly legal position of the Irish Roman Catholics, and such were the restrictions under which they lay in the reign of Charles II. The noble lords and the distinguished

---

[1] 27 Eliz. c. 2 (English).
[2] 14 and 15 Chas. II, c. 19, § 14.
[3] Rules made by the Lord Lieutenant and Council under the authority of 17 and 18 Chas. II, c. 2.
[4] 17 and 18 Chas. II, c. 2, § 36. [5] *Curry*, ii. 82.
[6] *Ib.* p. 84. [7] *Ib.* p. 93. [8] *Leland*, iii. 474.

commoners, who were now bargaining so closely in forty-two articles for their own broad lands,[1] and for the transport of the troops which were to lend them prestige in a foreign country, were content that this state of things should continue. After their first proposals on the 27th of September, they did not make a single effort to ameliorate the condition or to remove the restrictions under which those whom they were preparing to desert had long suffered. Had the Irish chiefs held out like brave men till the arrival of the French succours, and then demanded that a parliament should be called to ratify a real improvement in the position of the Roman Catholics, they would have been merely fulfilling a duty which they owed to a population which they themselves had rashly called to meet the dreadful risk of winning or losing all. Had Limerick been defended with the stubborn courage with which the northern farmers had defended the city of Derry, the whole subsequent history of the Irish Roman Catholics would have been different. But the unconquerable will which derives fresh energy from despair, the obstinate valour which does not know when it is beaten, were wanting to the Irish leaders. In the northern city to utter the word "surrender" was death to the speaker; in Limerick there was a race to capitulate. The defenders of Derry could not purchase a small fish for money, and dogs, cats, and vermin had become delicacies; the besieged in Limerick had two months' supplies, says Story, "of the finest French biscuit I ever tasted," and the city was not closed in on the Clare side until the very day before the parley was beaten. Famine, pestilence, and the strange diseases which an unwholesome diet and the stench from unburied bodies beget, had thinned the numbers and blackened the faces of the surviving citizens

---

[1] By the civil treaty the estates of the Irish officers in all the Irish garrisons were secured to them; this proviso was confirmed by the subsequent Act of Parliament.

of Derry; the soldiers of Limerick were healthy and well nurtured. Three months of such suffering as is to be found only in a beleaguered city had not quelled the spirit of the northern Protestants; twenty-seven days was the utmost limit of the endurance of the mock heroes who were strutting upon the Limerick stage, and declaring that they were fighting for their king, their country, and the freedom of their religion. To all who are acquainted with the stories of Derry, of Rochelle, and of Saragossa; to all brave men who are conscious to themselves what they are capable of doing and suffering for their country and their religion, the second defence of Limerick must ever appear to be a contemptible sham and not a reality.

It is vain to urge in defence of the Irish leaders that they relied on the hope that the king would be able to obtain from the Parliament further securities for the free exercise of the Roman Catholic religion. No one knew better than Sarsfield the folly of such expectations. In a political and religious crisis such as then existed, the wishes of a sovereign were certain to be neglected, and the policy of a king who was a foreigner and knew nothing of the country was sure to be examined, criticised, and opposed. The example of the English Legislature, which was then exasperated against the Roman Catholics, would naturally be followed by an Irish parliament which would consist of members whose estates had been confiscated, and who had themselves been condemned to death by a Roman Catholic assembly. Sarsfield and the other Irish commissioners knew well that it did not lie within the province of the executive to relax or dispense with general laws. Sarsfield had been a captain in King James's life-guards in England. He was in that country during the whole contest regarding the dispensing power. He was well aware of the extent of the royal authority and the limitations on the sovereign's powers. He knew that the King of England was of himself unable to touch one of the laws which affected the Irish Roman Catholics. Nor was Sarsfield alone in the negotiation of the treaty. He was supported by three distinguished lawyers, Sir Garret Dillon, Sir Theobald Butler,[1] and Colonel Brown, who were equally well acquainted with the power of the sovereign and the rights of the legislature. These gentlemen were easily satisfied. They were content with a single clause which in its first part was illusory and contained no promise of alleviation, and in its second merely contained an undertaking, the success of which depended on the approbation of a third party unknown and yet unborn. It is no wonder that Colonel Kelly exclaims against the treaty and declares that it was a marvel surpassing the capacity of man to understand how the Irish leaders came to conclude a peace "without conditions for their sacred bishops or obtaining security for the free exercise of their divine ceremonies."

But these leaders had resolved to desert the people whom they had called to arms, and were careless in what condition they left their brethren. A high authority has praised the conduct of the Irish chiefs in leaving their country at this juncture. "Whatever," says Sir Walter Scott, "our opinion may be of the cause for which the followers of James abandoned their country and fortunes, there can be but one sentiment concerning the courage and self-devotion with which they sacrificed their all to a sense of duty." But there is a higher self-devotion than following a king, or like well-endowed adventurers,—for their trains of soldiers were the capital of the Irish captains,—pushing their fortunes in a new country with delightful prospects of rank and promotion; and that is, to abide with one's own people; to console them under their afflictions; to share their sufferings; and with them to struggle into the full freedom of emancipation. I can see no difference in principle between the conduct of

[1] Solicitor-General to the Irish Government of James II.

Sarsfield and his companions who abandoned Ireland in 1691, and that of the French nobles who deserted their country in 1790. Sarsfield was the one man in Ireland whose remaining in the country would have been of infinite service to his co-religionists, and his retiring to a hostile kingdom aggravated most seriously the misfortunes of those who were left behind. Before leaving the country he declared publicly to his troops that they were going to France only to return to Ireland as a conquering army.[1] There can be very little doubt that the fear of such a return, and the existence of an Irish army on a hostile shore, ready to invade the country at a moment's notice, was one of the principal causes which prevented the full ratification of the Treaty of Limerick, and compelled the Irish Parliament to reduce the Roman Catholics to complete political impotence by penal enactments as to property and the tenure and acquisition of land. "If," was the consideration which was present to the minds of the members of the Irish Parliament, "we cannot prevent an invasion, we can at least lessen the power of the disaffected in the country to give aid to the invaders."

The sum total then of the only provision in the civil treaty, as far as an improvement in the condition of the Roman Catholics is concerned, was absolutely *nil*. In other words, they were to remain as they were. This provision, lame as it is, would have, if ratified by Parliament, secured them against the imposition of further disabilities. But this provision was by the twelfth article conditional on its confirmation by Parliament. The Irish commissioners acknowledge in the treaty that the consent of Parliament was necessary to its confirmation, otherwise the covenant to solicit its approval is unmeaning. It is clear that when they requested a parliamentary ratification, they did themselves in effect show that they considered such confirmation was required to

[1] Story, *Cont.* p. 259.

complete the treaty. The Irish commissioners were well aware that the Lords Justices were the delegates of the Crown and not of a parliament which was not in existence. They knew that it did not lie within the delegated powers of such officers to sanction provisions which might bind or hamper the legislative discretion of a future parliament, and therefore they only demanded a promise of the king's endeavours to have the treaty confirmed by that parliament. On the other hand, the Lords Justices were careful to act within their delegation. They did not undertake that parliament would confirm the treaty, nor did they even speak of the probability of that event. It would have been absurd for them to have promised on behalf of a future parliament which was sure to consist of members justly indignant with the oppression, spoliation, confiscation, and proscriptions, which they had suffered during the domination of the Roman Catholics.

That the king did keep his promise and did endeavour to mitigate the laws which pressed upon the Roman Catholics of Ireland is certain. From the moment the Treaty of Limerick was signed, he and his representatives, the Lords Justices, exerted the powers of government to indulge and protect that body in every possible way. The treaty was carried out as if it was binding and did not require the ratification of Parliament. Catholic gentlemen who had been in James's army were admitted to or continued in the commission of the peace; Catholic officers were restored into the army, and the oaths were altered to suit their consciences, that part which required them to renounce the jurisdiction of the Pope and of other foreign powers being left out;[1] the reversals of outlawries and attainders recommenced, and sixty-five great proprietors who were not within the articles of Limerick were

---

[1] Articles of impeachment of the Lords Justices, *Parliamentary History*, v. 817.

reinstated by the special favour of the Crown;[1] their estates were restored to twelve hundred and eighty-three persons who were adjudged to come within the Treaty of Limerick;[2] protections were granted to Roman Catholics whereby Protestants were hindered from their legal remedies.[3] The disputed clause in the treaty was, before ratification in Parliament, treated as binding, and under it many Catholics repossessed themselves of the estates which they had forfeited by their rebellion.[4] We are told by a Roman Catholic historian that during the first four years of William's reign "the Irish Catholics enjoyed the full and free exercise of their religion; they were protected in their persons and properties; their industry was encouraged, and under his mild and fostering administration the desolation of the late war began to disappear, and prosperity, peace, and confidence to smile once more on the country."[5]

The king had undertaken in the twelfth article to use his utmost endeavours to have the treaty ratified and confirmed in Parliament. This was therefore his first duty. The willingness or unwillingness of the Parliament to concede this would enable him to judge how far he could proceed in his intention to obtain further securities for the exercise of the Roman Catholic religion. A Parliament was accordingly summoned and met on the 5th of October 1692, a twelvemonth after the surrender of Limerick. A Bill was sent over from England for the confirmation of the Treaty of Limerick, and the members were told that they had nothing else to do but pass it and the other Government measures, inasmuch as their provisions had been "as well debated already as was needful."[6] It soon became evident, however, that the king and the Irish

---

[1] Report on Irish Forfeitures, *State Tracts*, ii. 709; and Address of the English Commons, *Parliamentary History*, v. 768.
[2] Report on Irish Forfeitures, *State Tracts*, ii. 711.
[3] Address of the English Commons, *Parl. History*, 5, 768.   [4] *Ib.*
[5] O'Conor's *History of the Irish Catholics*, pp. 116, 117.
[6] *Account of the Parliament in* 1692, Dublin, 1793.

Parliament took very different views of the policy which should be adopted for governing Ireland. The king was at a distance and knew nothing of the circumstances of the country. The lot of the members of the Parliament was to live among a people who outnumbered the Protestants by five to one, and who had, in two late rebellions, threatened them and their brethren not only with forfeiture and confiscation but with the extirpation of themselves and their religion. To confirm the articles of Limerick appeared to them the same thing as to sign away every guarantee of their lives and security.[1] They were deaf to every suggestion which emanated from the Crown. They threw out one of the money bills because it had not taken its rise in their house, and carried a resolution that it was the undoubted right of the Irish Commons to prepare and resolve the ways and means of raising money; they declared the Bill for confirming the Act of Settlement and Explanation to be a Bill "of such pernicious contexture as instead of confirming it would have unsettled the greatest part of the estates of the kingdom;"[2] they agreed to a report of a committee that the continuance of Papists in the army was of dangerous consequence; and they rejected the Mutiny Bill in resentment of the admission of such officers, though it had been specially recommended to their consideration by the Government. It was clear that there was no hope of getting the treaty ratified by a parliament in such a humour. The brief and stormy session of less than a month was closed with an angry rebuke from the Lord Lieutenant, who accused the Parliament of having invaded the prerogative of the Crown, and insisted that his rebuke should be inserted in the journals of the

---

[1] "The first article of which, if confirmed, would make popery an established religion, and the sixth would deprive all Protestants of their actions against the Papists, by whom they were plundered even while they lived in peace with them."—*Account of the Parliament in* 1692, Dublin, 1793. [2] *Ib.*

House. The Parliament was prorogued till April 1693, and finally, after a further prorogation, dissolved in September of the same year.

Two years were allowed to elapse before another Parliament was called in 1695. An interval of quiet was necessary to let the heats and passions on both sides cool down. The king again renewed his request that the Parliament should ratify the treaty as it stood, but he soon found that all his endeavours were ineffectual. Though he very unwillingly consented to give up the disputed clause in the treaty, and though to conciliate the Parliament he relinquished the power of reversing Irish outlawries,[1] the House was not to be brought over to his views. Induced, however, by the king, they entered upon the consideration how far they might in prudence ratify the treaty. They confirmed *sub modo* and with considerable qualifications some of the clauses which referred to individuals and certain classes of persons in existence at the time the treaty was made, and they also restored all the Irish officers in Limerick and the other Irish garrisons to their estates.[2] But beyond this they would not go. They passed over in silence the first and only clause which related to the Roman Catholics as a body, and by so doing they refused to confirm that clause. They saw that if they were to ratify it they would debar themselves from enacting any further restrictions which, in their legislative discretion, the circumstances of the times and of the kingdom might require. If, by a legislative enactment, they had confirmed the words contained in the first clause, viz. "that the Roman Catholics should continue to enjoy such privileges in the exercise of their religion as they had enjoyed in the reign of Charles II," they would have been bound by them;

---

[1] 9 Will. III, c. 5.
[2] "An Act for the confirmation of articles made at the surrender of the city of Limerick."—9 Will. III, c. 2.

and the imposition of further disabilities *might*[1] have been a violation, not of the treaty to which they were not a party, but of their own law recognising and adopting that treaty. But the Irish Parliament was resolved to keep its hands free from any obligation of this kind, and to make itself a party to the treaty only in such a manner as would leave its future discretion untrammelled. If then the Irish Parliament was not in the first instance a party to the treaty, as most certainly it was not, not being in existence when it was made; if the treaty was by express stipulation within its four corners, reserved for the consideration, and made subject to the approbation and confirmation of Parliament; and if that Parliament, after consideration of its terms, refused its approval and ratification, it is impossible to argue that the treaty was violated by the Parliament, or that the Parliament was restrained in any way from imposing on the Roman Catholics the restrictions which it afterwards imposed.

Nor was the treaty violated by the king. We have seen that William performed his part, and that what he undertook was loyally carried out. He observed every stipulation in that part of it which is known as the military articles, and which did not require the intervention of the Legislature. He ratified the civil treaty, as he was bound to do, within eight months from its being signed, but subject again in words to the approbation and confirmation of Parliament.[2]

[1] I say *might*, for it is clear that even if the first Parliament of William had ratified every clause in the treaty, subsequent Parliaments would not have been bound thereby. The safety of the state, a change in the circumstances of the kingdom, would justify any alteration in the laws. It is a maxim of our constitution that subsequent Parliaments are not bound by the decisions of earlier ones. But I am considering the matter on moral grounds and not as a special pleader.

[2] "And as to such parts thereof, for which an Act of Parliament shall be found to be necessary, we shall recommend the same to be made good by Parliament, and shall give our royal assent to any bill or bills that shall be passed by our two Houses of Parliament to that purpose."—Ratification by William, 24th February 1692.

He used his utmost endeavours to mitigate the condition of the Roman Catholics, and struggled to the best of his abilities to obtain from the Parliament the ratification and confirmation of the treaty as a whole.

It has never been stated by any Roman Catholic writer of authority that William himself violated the treaty. Even the Irish authors have done justice to the truth and honour of the king. O'Conor, in his *History of the Irish Catholics*, informs us that William, in pursuance of his stipulation, "had often recommended the ratification of the treaty to Parliament,"[1] a fact with which we are also acquainted from the preamble to the Act of the ninth of William. And when some of the Catholics appeared by counsel at the bar of the Irish Commons to oppose the proposed Act of Anne[2] in 1703, no allegation was made that the Treaty of Limerick had then been violated either by the king or any one else. All that was urged was, that the proposed Act against which they were petitioning *would*, if passed, infringe the treaty. But it was forgotten by Sir Theobald Butler, who appeared for the petitioners, that the civil treaty was conditional on the approbation and confirmation of the Parliament, and that it had never been confirmed by that body, though he was so rash as to affirm that it had been so ratified. He must have known that this general statement was unfounded, and that the Parliament had been careful not to ratify the treaty as it stood, but only such parts of it as to leave their future discretion uncontrolled by any recognition of the treaty as a whole.

The accusation of violating the treaty has been directed not against the king but against the Irish Parliament. The charge is that that body, by the Act of Anne in 1703 *to*

---

[1] *History of the Irish Catholics*, p. 136.
[2] 2 Anne, c. 6 — "An Act to prevent the further growth of Popery."

prevent the further growth of Popery, and by other subsequent Acts, violated rights which were secured by the treaty. There is no ground whatever for this accusation. The civil treaty was not absolute but conditional, both expressly in words and from the nature of the matters in it, on the approval of the Parliament; that body was not a party to it, and when the treaty was submitted to it for its consideration, the Legislature rejected the only clause which referred to the Roman Catholics in general. The Parliament had no share in the treaty save that it ratified certain articles in it which referred only to classes and persons in existence when the treaty was made. And having repudiated the only clause which referred to the body of the Roman Catholics, it is absurd to say that it violated that clause by subsequently imposing restrictions which it considered to be necessary.

But it may be urged that the Irish Parliament, though not a party to the treaty, was bound legally, or if not legally at least morally, to ratify the civil treaty. If this be so, the Irish Parliament is justly charged with a violation of it, or, more properly, with the violation of a treaty which, though concluded by the sovereign alone, was yet binding on it. This is a grave statement; let us examine what justice there is in it.

The doctrine that a Legislature is legally or constitutionally bound to ratify a treaty made by the executive, to which that Legislature is not a party and of which it disapproves, is a new one and a stranger to our system of law. Large as the power is which is lodged in the executive to declare war or to make treaties of peace, Parliament has always retained the privilege of controlling the exercise of such a power, and of showing its disapprobation either by refusing supplies for carrying on the war, or by declining to enact such laws as may be necessary to complete the peace. The argument that the Irish Parliament was bound to ratify whatever treaty the Crown had made with the Limerick garrison, and to pass an Act confirming that treaty without exercising its legislative discretion thereupon, proves too much. For let us suppose that William had chosen, in his ignorance of the country, to grant more favourable terms than those conceded by him. That he had agreed, for instance, to the public establishment of the church of the Roman Catholics, or that he had undertaken that all the laws against that body, from the Act of Uniformity downwards, should be swept away. Would any one gravely maintain that Parliament was bound to ratify such terms? Such a doctrine would deprive Parliament of all power of controlling the executive, and would degrade it into a mere machine for registering the acts of the sovereign. The Parliament undoubtedly possesses the right of refusing to ratify treaties made with foreign powers, and if so, it has at least an equal right of declining to confirm one made with subjects of the realm. It has this right, even in those cases where the treaty is absolute in its terms, and is not bound to confirm it, unless it meets with its approval. Much more has the Parliament this right when the treaty is conditional only, and expressly made subject to its confirmation. Inasmuch as the civil Treaty of Limerick was conditional and stipulated to be submitted to the Parliament for its approval and confirmation, it was the duty of the Irish Legislature to consider its terms, and if, in the exercise of its consultative discretion, the Parliament came to the conclusion that those terms were opposed to the interests of the nation, it was bound to reject them. This was not the first occasion on which the Irish Parliament refused to confirm a treaty made by its king. The Parliament of Charles II declined to ratify in the Act of Settlement the treaty and the engagements which the sovereign had entered into with the Irish in 1648.

Nor was the Irish Parliament morally bound to ratify the civil treaty. The only just way of judging actors in the past is to place ourselves, as far as we can, in their position, to look at their surroundings from their point of view, and to weigh and consider the circumstances of the kingdom and what appeared to be the obvious necessities of the times. Let us consider the sufferings which the members of the Parliament which refused to ratify all the treaty of Limerick had lately gone through; the dangers of the State; the probability of an invasion which would again throw Ireland into confusion; and the necessity of weakening the disaffected at home to prevent their giving aid to the invaders. If we do so, no impartial man can deny that the Irish Parliament was, according to the views and standard of those times, justified in following the example of England, and in reducing the Irish Roman Catholics to political impotency. If the Irish Parliament sinned in acting as it did, it sinned under infinitely greater provocations than the English people, from whose legislation every enactment in the Irish penal code was borrowed. And if we extend our views beyond England we shall find that the conduct of the Irish Parliament towards the Roman Catholics was complete and absolute toleration when compared with the bloody and merciless persecution of their Protestant subjects by the Catholic Governments of France, Spain, Savoy, and Austria.

1. Within the fifty years which preceded the surrender of Limerick, two universal rebellions of the whole body of Irish Roman Catholics against the Protestants had taken place, in 1641 and 1689. On both these occasions the attention of England was called away from Ireland on account of political crises of her own. The opportunities were eagerly seized on by the Irish Roman Catholics to separate from England, and to destroy the Protestant interest in Ireland. The horrors and barbarities which marked the insurrection of 1641 have been palliated,

denied, or minimised by some *modern* Roman Catholic writers,[1] but they were admitted and deplored by every contemporaneous Catholic of position or authority — by such men as Lord Clanricarde, Lord Castlehaven, Owen Roe O'Neil,[2] Father Walsh,[3] Father Caron,[4] and George Leyburn,[5] chaplain to Henrietta Maria. "It is a fact," says the Rev. Charles O'Conor, a Catholic clergyman and historian, "as certain as any in history, that they [the Irish rebels of 1641] were taught to expect impunity *only* from extirpation;[6] fearing that their men might disperse and throw themselves on the king's mercy, the leaders resolved that all should be equally guilty; that they should embark in wickedness beyond redemption." During this rebellion the crown of Ireland was hawked about Europe by the Irish leaders and offered to any foreign prince that would take the kingdom under his protection.[7] This rebellion cost six hundred thousand lives, more than a third of the whole population of Ireland, and reduced the country to a desert.

The rebellion of 1689 was as universal as that of 1641.

[1] In 1645, in the middle of the rebellion, a book was published by an Irish Jesuit, Connor O'Mahony, in which he congratulates his Roman Catholic countrymen on having slaughtered 150,000 of the Protestants between the years 1641 and 1645. This book was condemned by the Supreme Council at Kilkenny in 1648. The Nuncio, Rinuccini, attempted to save it from condemnation. It would thus appear that the archbishop approved the sentiments, and believed in the estimates, of the book.

[2] General of the Irish Celtic army.

[3] Author of the *History of the Irish Remonstrance*, etc.

[4] Author of *Loyalty Asserted*. Ware enumerates seven works of his and speaks highly of him.

[5] Sent on a political mission to Ireland by the king.

[6] *Historical Address*, pt. ii. p. 243.

[7] When in 1661 deputies were sent over to England by the Irish Roman Catholics to plead for their estates, the document, offering the crown of Ireland to any Catholic prince that would take it, was produced. It was signed, among others, by the deputies, who could not deny their signatures. When Charles II saw the paper he was indignant and "sharply reproved the deputies for daring to appear before him" with so much guilt upon them, "and forbade them for ever his presence and court."—Harris, *William III*, i. 252.

"It is notorious," says a report of the English House of Commons in 1693,[1] that not an Irishman who was in Ireland during the late rebellion and capable of being guilty thereof, either by being actually in arms or by aiding, abetting, and assisting the rebels, is innocent." But the proceedings, which were in this outbreak aimed at the destruction of the Protestants, were of a different nature from those adopted in 1641. Legal chicanery was called in to aid open violence in the field. A Roman Catholic Parliament, as we have seen, was convened in Dublin on the 7th of May 1689, and passed Acts which were aimed at the destruction of the Protestants. One of these Acts repealed the Act of Settlement, and at one blow transferred twelve million acres of land from Protestant proprietors to Irish rebels. Another was the Act of Attainder. By this latter Act the whole Protestant peerage, gentry, and trading classes of Ireland were at one sweep (without a crime—for they were bound by the law of Ireland to refuse allegiance to a sovereign dethroned by the English Parliament,[2] and without the hope of pardon—for this prerogative was taken away from James by the Act) condemned to death. In the Parliament which was asked to adopt as its own Act the civil treaty of Limerick, there was probably not a single individual who had not been doomed by the Roman Catholic assembly to the scaffold or the block; whose lands had not been taken from him; and whose estate had not been turned from a garden to a wilderness.

2. When the question of confirming the civil treaty was debated and considered in Ireland, there was a large Irish army ready to embark and to invade either England or Ireland according to the orders it should receive. Twenty

---

[1] *Journals of the House of Commons*, xi. 56.
[2] By the Irish Act 33 Henry VIII, c. 1, the King of England is, immediately and without the sanction of an Irish Act, King of Ireland.

thousand[1] embodied and disciplined Irish troops in the service of France kept both the English and Irish Parliament in a state of constant alarm. In 1692, a few months after the surrender of Limerick, an invasion was actually prepared. A camp was formed in Normandy, and all the Irish regiments were assembled there under the command of Sarsfield to take part in it. James himself went down to the coast and witnessed the sea-fight which put an end for the present to his hopes of returning to England. In Ireland it was observed "that multitudes of the Roman Catholics quitted their habitations, ran from province to province to hold consultations together, and were in continual fluctuation of action and spirits—certain indications that they were preparing for some great design."[2] In 1696 another invasion was planned. The Duke of Berwick was sent to England to ascertain what force the Roman Catholics could bring into the field, and to assure them that his father would join them with 12,000 veterans. Two regiments of horse were prepared in London, and eight of horse and foot were levied in Lancashire, the most Catholic portion of England. Contemporaneously with these plans for invasion and insurrection, a succession of assassination plots exasperated and alarmed the English and Irish Parliaments. Was it any wonder that these legislatures regarded the Roman Catholics as enemies that could not be appeased or conciliated, and that they resolved to reduce them to political insignificance? But the Irish Parliament had a justification for their conduct which that of England had not. "Fifty-two rebellions," it is declared in a report of the English Commons, "which the Irish have been guilty of, may sufficiently evince that nothing can reconcile the implacable hatred of them to the British nation; and

[1] James II says in his Memoirs "near 30,000 men."—Clarke's *Life of James II*, ii. 465.
[2] Dalrymple, *Memoirs of Great Britain and Ireland*, iii. 229.

the only way of securing that kingdom to the crown of England is the putting it out of the power of the Irish again to rebel, gentle means having hitherto always proved ineffectual; and the favour they received after being conquered in one rebellion always laid a foundation for the next."[1]

3. The Irish Parliament had before their eyes what they believed to be the sad proofs of what their fate would be if a Roman Catholic Government were reinstated in Ireland. No such Government could be restored without the help of Louis XIV, the friend and patron of James, to whose assistance the Irish Roman Catholics had long looked. The conduct of this sovereign to his own subjects enabled the Irish Protestants to foresee what their position would be under a Government supported and directed by him.[2] Six years before the surrender of Limerick Louis had violated every feeling of mercy and policy and revoked the Edict of Nantes. The dragonnades followed, and a ferocious soldiery was let loose to devastate and depopulate a quarter of France. Thousands of both sexes and of every age were slaughtered or done to death in some shape or other. Murder, torture, rape, every form of cruelty, were called in to add to the numbers of the converts to the Roman Catholic Church. In less than six weeks eighty thousand of the persecuted Protestants abjured.[3] "From torture to abjuration," says St. Simon, "and from that to the communion, there was only twenty-four hours' distance, and executioners were the conductors of the converts." At the period we are speaking of, there were in the streets of London,

---

[1] 12th of January 1693. *Journals of the English Commons*, xi. 57.

[2] "King James had the scheme of the revocation [of the Edict of Nantes] imparted to him before it was issued; he expressed the greatest delight at it."—Ranke, *History of England*, iv. 267, translation.

[3] 60,000 in Basse-Guienne, 20,000 in Haute-Guienne.—Martin, *Histoire de France*, xiv. 43.

and scattered through the towns of England, besides those who had gone to the colonies or come to Ireland, upwards of thirty thousand[1] French Protestants of every rank, from the noble to the artisan, who had been driven from their country for professing the religion which the Irish Parliament professed.

[1] "Report of the English House of Commons, 13th February 1691;" *Journals of the House*, x. 666. Mazure makes the number 50,000. Michelet puts it at 80,000.

SECTION II

THE CHARGE OF INTOLERANCE AGAINST THE IRISH PROTESTANT PARLIAMENT

It was certainly not from any feeling of religious intolerance that the Irish Parliament refused to confirm the Treaty of Limerick. Nothing can be more unfair than the conduct of some English authors who point to the Irish penal code as the essence of intolerance, without stating that there was not a single penalty, disability, or restriction in that code which was not derived from their own legislation. The Whig writers, who are able to see no salvation without or beyond their own narrow and limited bounds, and whose undisturbed self-complacence amuses while it irritates their readers, are the chief offenders in this respect. Burke describes the Irish system as "an unparalleled code of oppression," and Macaulay speaks of the Irish Statute Book as "being polluted by intolerance as barbarous as that of the dark ages." If these writers had made themselves acquainted with the jurisprudence of England, they would have learned that the penal code of their own country was more severe than that of Ireland. They would have discovered that many enactments borrowed from the English code had been mitigated and softened down before they were adopted by the Irish Parliament. Thus in England it was death for a priest to receive a convert into the bosom of the Church of Rome; in Ireland the penalty was imprisonment only. In England the legislature attempted—happily without avail—to prevent a Roman Catholic succeeding to the estate of his father;[1] in Ireland this was softened into a descent of the estate in gavelkind. In England no Roman Catholic could purchase a lease or term of the shortest duration; in Ireland Roman Catholics were allowed to acquire terms for thirty-one years. Even the law which excluded Irish Roman Catholics from Parliament was passed, not by the Irish, but by the English Legislature.[2] An Irish Protestant may recall with pride and satisfaction the fact that of the three governments in the empire the Irish Parliament was the first to relax the penal laws against the Roman Catholics.

And what a difference existed between the position of the Protestants in England and those of Ireland, and the respective dangers which threatened them! If it be true, as most assuredly it is, that nothing but hard necessity and the imperative law of self-preservation can justify penal enactments against our fellow-subjects, what justification can England offer for such enactments compared to the thousand times stronger one which the Irish Parliament can produce? In England the Roman Catholics were a small and inconsiderable minority, the Protestants being more than a hundred to one.[3] In Ireland the Catholics formed an overwhelming

---

[1] 11 and 12 Will. III, c. 4, § 4, 1700. The Act was evaded in two ways. "First, there being in all families a gradation of age among the several heirs to the same estates, it happened that though the person who was come to the age of eighteen did not take the oaths prescribed by the law, yet the title of the Protestant heir remained undecided as long as any next popish heir was under age. Secondly (and this was the main inconveniency), it lying by that clause upon the next heir to him who at the age of eighteen refused to declare himself a Protestant, to prove that he had not made that declaration, it was impossible for the next heir to prove such a negative."—*Parliamentary History*, vi. 514.

[2] 3 William and Mary, c. 2, § 5, 1691.

[3] James II in his Memoirs estimates them as "at least two hundred to one."—Clarke's *Life of James II*, ii. 442.

majority, being to the Protestants as at least five to one. In England the greater portion of the Catholic secular clergy— I do not speak of the missionary regulars who were the real authors of the early penal laws—and of the Catholic laity had long been loyal; in Ireland both the priests and their people were implacably opposed to the Government and the Protestant religion. A perpetual crop of rebellions had not taught the English Protestants to distrust their Roman Catholic fellow-subjects, nor inculcated the necessity of binding them hand and foot to keep them quiet. The English Protestants had not seen themselves disarmed by their adversaries, excluded from the army, and exposed in their defenceless state to the outrages of an uncivilised and fanatical peasantry which did not even understand the English tongue. They had not witnessed their Courts of Justice handed over to their declared enemies, and the whole executive power in the country transferred to their foes. The members of the English Parliament who passed in 1700 the Statute *for the further preventing the growth of Popery*,[1] the model and precedent of the similarly-named Irish Act,[2] had not been condemned to death for obeying the laws of their country by a Roman Catholic Parliament sitting in their capital. They had not been driven into exile from their native land; nor had their estates, their demesnes, and their pleasant homes been taken from them and given over to others. Yet all these things had taken place in Ireland in the late rebellion of 1689; infinitely worse things had happened in 1641. If we consider this condition of affairs and are able to comprehend all that it means and includes, and if we compare the position of the Irish Protestants, few in number and scattered among a hostile population, with that of their English brethren dwelling in peace and security

---

[1] 11 and 12 Will. III, c. 4 [English].
[2] 2 Anne, c. 6, 1703.

among their friends, we shall be almost tempted at the first view to believe that the penal laws were, in England, the results of a childish panic, and that in Ireland they were the consequences of a justifiable and necessary policy.

The narrator or historian who, like the Irish Roman Catholic writers, limits his views to one country without taking into account contemporaneous events in neighbouring nations, conceals half the truth, and blindfolds while he misleads his readers. Ireland was not so remote as not to be powerfully influenced by the movements which took place in other parts of Europe, particularly in those with which she had been long and intimately acquainted. France and Spain, the favourite resorts of disaffected Irishmen, were the two powers which were best known to Irish Roman Catholics and embodied their idea of what a Government should be. It is instructive to consider the position of the Protestant subjects in those countries and to compare it with that of the Roman Catholics under a Protestant Irish Parliament. I do not use the language of exaggeration or overstep the limits of literal truth when I say, that the position of the Irish Roman Catholics at the worst period of the penal laws was a *paradise* when compared with the condition of the Protestants in France, Spain, Austria, and Savoy, at the same period. Though the Protestants in these countries were, like the Roman Catholics of England, an inconsiderable minority, and a body from which no secular danger was to be feared, they were persecuted with a ferocious cruelty which was aimed at their extermination. There is a sure test by which we can determine whether religious enactments are or are not persecuting laws. If such enactments are politically necessary, if they are required by the safety of the State, then, provided they are not more severe than need requires, they cease to be persecuting laws, however much their necessity may be deplored. If we try the Irish penal laws by this test we must acknowledge that there was a justification for their enactment. But there was absolutely no justification for the contemporaneous laws against the Protestants in France, Spain, Savoy, and the dominions of the House of Austria. In France the Protestants had remained perfectly quiet for two generations,[1] ever since the taking of Rochelle and the settlement effected by Richelieu. Many of them had been called to office by Colbert; many of them also had been employed by Mazarin, who even appointed one of them, Hervart, Comptroller General of the Finances.. During the life of Mazarin there was no excitement among them and no question of religion arose. At the time when their persecution began, the French Protestants were hardly distinguishable from their fellow-subjects, except by the greater purity of their lives and morals,[2] and were sinking quietly and gradually into the general body of the French people.

Long before its formal revocation the Edict of Nantes had been violated. The persecution of the Protestants commenced immediately after the death of Mazarin in 1661. They were forbidden to sing their Psalms even in their own houses. Their children, at the age of seven, were invited by law to renounce their families, to declare themselves Catholics, and to exact an allowance from their parents; or they were taken from them and distributed in convents or other institutions. Many of their churches were razed to the ground, eighty in one diocese alone, and their endowments confiscated

---

[1] "Nulle injustice, nul outrage ne réussissait à lasser la patience de nos protestants. Il était difficile de trouver à la persécution quelque prétexte politique."—Michelet, *Louis XIV et la révocation de l'édit de Nantes.* "Cependant apres la prise de la Rochelle et l'edit de grace les guerres civiles cessérent, et il n'y eut plus que disputes. On imprimait de part et d'autre de ces gros livres qu'on ne lit plus."—Voltaire, *Du calvinisme sous Louis XIV.*

[2] "L'explication est donnée par les plus sages catholiques et les mieux informés, les gouverneurs, les intendants. Ils temoignent qui, ni pour les mœurs, ni pour l'instruction, les catholiques ne soutenaient la comparaison avec les protestants, ni les prêtres avec les ministres."
—Michelet, *Louis XIV et la révocation de l'édit de Nantes.*

to Roman Catholic uses. Decree succeeded decree against the Protestants with frightful rapidity.[1] An ordinance was published in 1681 declaring that it was a mistake to suppose that the king forbade the maltreatment of the Protestants. The natural consequences of such a decree ensued. Many Protestants were put to death at Grenoble and Bordeaux. Massacres were committed in the Vivarais and Cevennes. The dragonnades commenced, and the effect was so terrible that entire towns declared themselves catholic. Thus the city of Nimes was converted within twenty-four hours, and Montauban and many other places after a few days. A universal terror preceded the red uniform and the high caps of the dragoons, who committed every kind of outrage and excess. Colbert, who knew the value to France of the industry and intelligence of the Protestants, at last appealed to the king, and the dragonnades were for a time suspended. But this illustrious man died in 1683, and with him died the last hopes of the Protestants of France. It was resolved to revoke the edict of Nantes. The king signed its repeal on the 17th of October 1685, and the decree of revocation was registered on the 22d of the same month.

By this fatal Act the martyrdom of a whole people was decreed, and industrial France was delivered up to military execution. Open and merciless war was declared against every Protestant man, woman, and child in France, while at the same time the frontiers were closed so that the victims could not escape. The penalty of death was imposed on emigration, and the informer who denounced an intending emigrant was rewarded with half his possessions. It was a hunt of the Protestants in an enclosed arena, where every avenue of escape was barred. The house of every Protestant

---

[1] Après la trève de Ratisbonne, les déclarations et arrêts hostiles au Protestantisme se succedèrent avec une rapidité effrayante."—Martin, *Histoire de France.*

became the scene of a tragedy. Women were outraged,[1] young girls were whipt by soldiers to convert them, and every child of five years of age was torn from its mother.[2] All, says a French historian, which man can suffer without immediate death, was inflicted on the Protestants. All the diabolical inventions of robbers for the extortion of money from their captives were had recourse to by the soldiers to make conversions. Fire was applied to the feet of some of the sufferers; others were flogged; others hung up by their extremities till they abjured. Mothers were tied to their bedposts while their starving infants were withheld from the nourishment of the breast till the acknowledgment of conversion was made.[3] Nor was the penalty of death absent. The stake, the wheel, and the gibbet had their multitudes of innocent victims; and the galleys, a fate worse than death, were filled with Protestant ministers. Nothing was wanting to the immolation of a whole community. To keep the Protestants, who had been forcibly converted, from straying from the Catholic fold, those of them who reverted to the faith of their fathers were burnt alive, and those who refused

---

[1] "Tout était en fait permis aux soldats sauf le viol et le meurtre, et encore cette restriction ne fut-elle pas toujours respectée; d'ailleurs beaucoup de malheureux moururent ou demeurèrent estropiés des suites des traitements qu'ils avaient subis, et les tortures obscenes infligées aux femmes ne différaient guère du dernier outrage que par une perversité plus raffinée."—Martin, *Histoire de France*. "Mais le viol était defendu, quelle moquerie! On ne punit personne, même quand il fut suivi de meurtre. On eût soin de loger les officiers ailleur que les soldats, de peur qu'ils ne les gênassent."—MICHELET.

[2] "Un édit de janvier 1686 ordonna que les enfants de cinq a seize ans fussent enlevés à leurs parents hérétiques et remis à des parents catholiques, ou s'ils n'en avaient pas, à des catholiques désignés par les juges."—MARTIN.

[3] "Toutes les inventions diaboliques des *routiers* du moyen âge pour extorquer de l'or à leurs captifs furent renouvelées çà et là pour arracher des conversions: on *chauffa* les pieds, on donna l'estrapade, on suspendit les patients par les extremités; on lia de jeunes mères aux colonnes de leur lit pendant que leur enfant à la mamelle se tordait de faim sous leurs yeux."—Martin, *Histoire de France*, xiv. 50.

to receive the sacrament at the hour of death, according to the Roman form, were denied six feet of their native soil to cover their remains. Their bodies were drawn naked on a hurdle and thrown into the public sewer, there to be devoured by obscene vermin.[1] As if to show to foreign Protestant Governments that the persecution was the result of a universal Catholic conspiracy against the Protestant religion, and to shut out the Roman Catholic subjects in their dominions from the hopes of toleration, the head of the Church of Rome, in 1686, celebrated the revocation of the edict of Nantes by a public and solemn Te Deum.

Can the word "life," asks Michelet, be applied to the existence passed by the French Protestants after the revocation of the edict of Nantes? Yes, it was life, is the answer, but it was the life of a hunted hare, trembling with ears erect at every rustle, and momentarily expecting the approach of the destroyer. Even the events, births and marriages, which bring joy and gladness into families, served but to renew the fears and anguish of the Protestants, who performed every ceremony of their religion at the risk of the galleys. The Protestant wife lamented when she became aware that she was about to become a mother, for she knew well the long agony of affliction which awaited her offspring, and that Protestants were regarded as worse than infidels and more dangerous than mad dogs. The condition of the French Protestants, though somewhat alleviated by the improvement in manners, remained unaltered till the opening of the great revolution. Yet the spirit of fanaticism was not dead; it slumbered merely, and the slightest suspicion was sufficient to revive it, as the misfortunes of the Calas family in 1762 only too surely demonstrated.[2]

[1] Quelques-uns qui rejetérent l'hostie après l'avoir reçue, furent condamnés à être brulés vifs. Les corps de ceux qui ne voulaient pas recevoir les sacrements à la mort étaient trainés sur la claie et jetés a la voirie."—Voltaire, *Siècle de Louis XIV.*

[2] At the succession of Louis XVI Turgot endeavoured to have

In the presence of such a scene of calamities as this, the complaints of the Irish Roman Catholic writers, that their co-religionists were excluded from public employment—that a change was made in the devolution of landed property—or that a disobedient son could alter his father's fee into a life estate, fall upon our ears like idle and trifling declamation. The French Protestants had not deserved their exclusion from the rights of citizenship by a perpetuity of rebellions; they were loyal and well affected to the State. Yet compare their condition under a Roman Catholic Government with that of the irreconcilable Irish Roman Catholics under a Protestant Parliament. There was in Ireland a priest in every parish, registered by order of the Government and under its protection. The Irish Roman Catholic was free, though there were laws in the statute book against his religion, to serve his God according to his convictions. He might build places of worship and attend them openly in perfect security. His person was at his own disposal, and he might transplant himself and his industry to a foreign country. His family and home were sacred. The laws were not interpreted to him and executed against him by a ferocious and fanatical soldiery opposed to his belief. The recognised Primate of his church, as if to proclaim the toleration of the Government, resided in the capital and within the shadow of the Castle. In France every Protestant church had been razed to the ground and its endowments and funds transferred to Catholic uses. Every Protestant minister had been banished at a notice of fifteen days, and his return forbidden on pain of death. All the ceremonies of the Protestant church were performed at the risk of the galleys—a punishment in comparison with which death itself was a release. It was death for the French

the clause which bound the King of France to exterminate the heretics in his dominions removed from the coronation oath. Turgot's endeavour was successfully opposed by the French clergy.—Tissot's *Life of Turgot.*

Protestants to assemble *in any place* to exercise their religion, and death to fly the country where they were doomed to such suffering. Every Protestant child was required to be baptized by a Catholic priest, and at the age of five years was taken from its mother.[1] The comparative toleration which was refused by a Roman Catholic Government to its own kindred and blood, to subjects whose only desire was to live in peace in the land of their fathers, and who spoke the French tongue, was granted by an Irish Protestant Legislature to a half-civilised people who, by rebellion after rebellion, had shown themselves its implacable enemies; who had lately in their Parliament condemned the Protestant nobility and gentry to confiscation and death; and who were aliens to it in language and blood. The toleration of the Protestant Legislature of Ireland was, considering the standard of the times and its own dangerous position in the midst of a hostile population, as remarkable as it was premature and unknown to the neighbouring nations. It was the first awakening, the early development, of that spirit which conceded complete toleration in 1793, and which has since matured into the lofty indifference of modern Great Britain to the variations of dogma and ritual.

A few words will suffice with respect to Spain. Life, under such conditions as I have described, was allowed to the Protestants in France, but bare life was denied them in Spain. In the latter country they were hunted and exterminated like wolves or other wild animals. The possession of a forbidden book, or the deposition of another under torture, was sufficient to consign a Protestant to the flames. Recantation did

[1] "L'énlèvement des enfants mit le dernier sceau à la persécution. L'édit de révocation avait seulement statué que les enfants à naître seraient élevés dans la religion catholique. Un édit de janvier 1686 ordonna que les enfants de cinq à seize ans fussent enlevés à leurs parents hérétiques et remis a des parents catholiques, ou s'ils n'en avaient pas, à des catholiques désignès par les juges."—Martin, *Histoire de France*, xiv. 51.

not save the abjuring victim, for the Government and its instrument, the Inquisition, wished to strike a general and preventive terror into the whole nation. Nor was the absence of evidence against suspects any security, for they were tortured till they informed against themselves or against their friends and relations. Death itself did not put an end to the vengeance of the Inquisition. If subsequent evidence, even the testimony of a tortured prisoner, was forthcoming, the memory of the dead was declared to be infamous, his house was razed to the ground, his property was confiscated and his bones were dug up and committed to the flames. It is repulsive to pursue the loathsome subject. One fact alone is sufficient to reveal to us the spirit which existed in Spain. The fires of persecution were kept alive up to 1781. During the *eighteenth* century upwards of sixteen hundred victims were burnt alive for entertaining opinions differing from those of the Spanish Church.

In the mountains of Savoy, on the borders of Piedmont and Dauphiné, there had long existed one of the most ancient Protestant churches in the world. This church had often passed through the fire of persecution, and had been for many generations fed and nurtured on the blood of its martyrs.[1] At the period we are speaking of, three of the high valleys, St. Martin, Perouse, and Lucerne, had obtained from the Government of Savoy toleration for their religion. When the dragonnades had penetrated to Dauphiné, the Protestants of Briançon and Pignerol took refuge among the peaceful inhabitants of these valleys. Louis XIV was indignant that these exiles should find an asylum with the brethren of their faith. He ordered the Duke of Savoy to occupy the valleys with his troops and to convert the Vaudois. The Duke

---

[1] Readers will remember Milton's words recording the persecutions of this people at another period—

"Avenge, O Lord, Thy slaughtered saints whose bones
Lie scattered on the Alpine mountains cold," etc.

published an ordinance banishing the French refugees from his territories. But this did not satisfy Louis, whose conduct at this time was a dreadful prognostic to the Irish Protestants of what was in store for them should a Roman Catholic Government be restored with the aid of the French king. Accordingly, at the instigation of Louis, the duke, by an edict of the 1st of February 1686, prohibited the exercise of the reformed faith, and ordered that the Protestant schools should be closed upon pain of death. All Protestant ministers, schoolmasters, and the French refugees, were directed under the same penalty to leave Piedmont within fifteen days. To carry out the persecution Louis offered the duke a body of four thousand French troops, and they and the Piedmontese soldiers invaded at the same time the three valleys. Those of St. Martin and Lucerne were forced by the French troops, who committed unheard-of atrocities. Mutilation of the unfortunate Protestants was a favourite amusement of the soldiers. Some of the inhabitants were burnt alive at once, others were burnt more methodically, joint by joint, at each refusal to abjure. Women were slaughtered, and young children were hurled down the precipices, the soldiers laughing at the bounds and ricochets of the bodies of the victims. While these things were being done by the French soldiers, the Piedmontese troops entered the valley of Perouse, and having induced the unhappy Protestants by false promises to lay down their arms, massacred at Tour three thousand old men, women, and children. More than ten thousand of the young and able-bodied men were bound and sent to Turin, from whence they were afterwards distributed through the prisons of Piedmont, where the greater part of them perished from bad treatment and misery.[1]

---

[1] The details of this persecution are to be found in Martin's *Histoire de France*, vol. xiv.; and in Michelet, *Louis XIV et la révocation de l'édit de Nantes.*

The dragonnades were not peculiar to France. Austria can also lay claim to having made use of this means of converting the Protestants. In 1672 the Austrian dragonnades against the reformed in Hungary commenced. We have the details of this persecution, not from the records of the Protestants only, but also from the official documents of the Viennese Cabinet, which Michiels has examined and made use of. Roman Catholic bishops, each with a train of three or four hundred dragoons, and attended by a squadron of Jesuits, perambulated the country. As soon as the motley horde arrived at a town or village, the inhabitants were collected, a Jesuit declaimed a sermon, the soldiers levelled their carbines, and the place was converted.[1] The obstinate were banished, their property confiscated, and Jesuits were installed in the churches, schools, and manses, which had been built by the Protestants at their own charges. But, as is usual in such cases, the persecution waxed warmer and fiercer as it proceeded. On the 5th of May 1675 all the Protestant pastors and schoolmasters were summoned to appear before a Catholic tribunal at Pressburg. Those of them who did not obey the summons were instantly condemned and a price set upon their heads. Four hundred obeyed and attended. They were charged with innumerable crimes, but the principal heads of accusation imputed to them neglect in worshipping the saints, insults to the Virgin Mary by comparing her to their own wives, trampling under foot the Holy Sacrament and venerable body of Jesus. All were declared guilty of high treason. The condemned were required to sign one of two documents. By one the signatory swore to abandon his religious duties and to be faithful to the prince, and in return he might remain in the country; by the other the signer undertook to leave his native land never to return. Both documents were confessions of guilt, and rendered the person

[1] Michiels's *Secret History of the Austrian Government*, p. 140.

signing liable to the penalties prescribed by the laws against heretics. A hundred ministers signed one or other of the documents. On the rest sentence of death was pronounced. But as the Government was ashamed to execute so many, they were disposed of in various ways. Some were sent to the State prisons, where they were loaded with chains and employed in disgusting work; others were sold as convicts, and others were sent to the galleys at Naples, Venice, or Trieste.[1]

In 1687 took place the long-continued butchery of Eperies, which lasted nine months. A court was established at this place, presided over by Antonio Caraffa, cousin of the apostolic Nuncio Cardinal Caraffa, and a man well fitted to carry out the threat of the emperor that he would take Hungary captive, and make her first mendicant and then Catholic.[2] A scaffold was erected in the market-place, and thirty executioners in green liveries obeyed the orders of Caraffa. The tortures inflicted and the murders committed during these nine months are almost incredible. The details are so frightful that the historian, Michiels, is obliged to apologise for producing them. Yet, says he, the facts of history must not be concealed: "let us then have the courage to be present, without giving way, at the tortures of the Hungarian patriots and reformers." It is not necessary here to recall the hideous story. It is sufficient for us to know that every kind of torment known to the wild Huron or the Turk was resorted to at Eperies. The stake, the wheel, impalement, laceration, red-hot pincers, the introduction of wires at a white heat into

[1] Twenty-eight of these martyrs, all that remained alive at Naples, were claimed and released by Admiral Ruyter in 1676. As late as 1731, 30,000 Protestants were expelled from Salzburg and driven into exile by the Austrian Government. Those who read these lines will recollect Goethe's "Hermann und Dorothea," the incidents of which are founded on this exodus.

[2] "Faciam Hungariam captivam, postea mendicam, deinde Catholicam."

the natural passages of the body, all the cruel inventions of man in his most savage mood, were made use of. The Hungarians found such arguments to be irresistible, and all who did not fly the country were converted to the Roman Catholic faith.[1]

Such was the scene of persecution and horror which Catholic Europe presented to the eyes of the Protestant Parliaments of England and Ireland, and which convinced those bodies that there was a universal conspiracy against Protestant opinions and Protestant Governments. Can we wonder at this conviction? Will any one presume to say at this day that such a conspiracy did not exist, either openly acknowledged and conducted by the Jesuits, or acquiesced in and helped forward by Roman Catholics in general?[2] We must remember too that at this time the Roman Court and the Roman Catholic clergy of Ireland still clung to the doctrine that it lay within the power of the Pope to dethrone sovereigns and to transfer to others the allegiance of their subjects:—a doctrine which led directly to the belief which was general among the English and Irish Protestants that the Roman Catholic religion was inconsistent with the existence of their own Governments.[3]

---

[1] "Grâce aux livres des exécuteurs, grâce aux lettres de Léopold, nous savons les petits moyens qui opérèrent ces œuvres pieux. Des ministres brulés vifs a feu lent, des femmes empalees au fer rouge, des troupeaux d'hommes vendus aux galères turques et venitiennes, voilà ce qui fit le miracle. Les Hongrois trouvèrent ces arguments des jesuites irresistibles. Tout ce qui ne s'enfuit pas du pays fut touché et sentit la grace."—Michelet, *Louis XIV et la révocation de l'édit de Nantes.*

[2] Catholic France, as a whole, approved of the revocation of the edict of Nantes.

[3] It is certain that this doctrine and its propagation by the missionary regulars, such as Parsons, were the *sole* causes of the enactment of the early penal laws. "It will be found on dispassionate inquiry," says the Rev. Charles O'Conor, "that the penal laws were enacted not against any one article of the Catholic faith, but for putting away all usurped powers and authorities," etc. "Had these [foreign]

As late as 1666 the Irish Roman Catholic clergy, in their synod in Dublin, refused to sign the "Loyal Remonstrance," which abjured this doctrine, and the Papal Nuncio at Brussels, De Vecchiis, condemned the Remonstrance because it denied the deposing power of the Pope. Irish writers and declaimers would do well to ponder on these things, and, before they rail against the intolerance of the Irish Parliament, to raise their eyes beyond the confines of their own country, and consider both the contemporaneous events in neighbouring nations and the irreconcilable disloyalty of their own clergy and laity. The members of the Irish Parliament would have been angels if they had acted differently from what they did, and conceded more to their Roman Catholic countrymen; and we are fools to listen to accusations of intolerance against men in their position, surrounded by dangers which menaced themselves, their posterity, and their religion, and who saw nothing around them but the merciless persecution of their Protestant brethren by the Roman Catholic Governments of Europe.

seminaries never existed, we had not heard of the seditious doctrines which I have mentioned, nor should we have been oppressed by the subsequent cruel laws enacted against our religion."—Sir JOHN THROCKMORTON. "Had these men [the English clergy who retired to the continent] remained at home, patient of present evils and submissive, as far as might be, to the laws; had they continued the practice of their religion in retirement and distributed without clamour instruction to those that claimed it, the rigour of the Legislature would soon have relaxed; no jealousy would have been excited, and no penal statutes, we may now pronounce, would have entailed misfortunes upon them and their successors."—Rev. JOSEPH BERINGTON.

APPENDIX

I

TWO COLUMNS OF NAMES FROM THE LIST OF PERSONS ATTAINTED BY THE IRISH PARLIAMENT

William Aldington and Richard Silver, all late of the county of Waterford and Cork.
Henry Brady of Tomgraney, in the county of Clare, Gent.
Richard Pickett of Clonmel, in the county of Tipperary, Esq.
John Lovett, Esq.
—— Castle, Gent.
Joseph Ruttorne, Gent.
Thos. Valentine, Gent.
George Clark, Gent.
John Bright, Gent.
George Clarke, Gent.
Thomas Chimmicks, Gent.
William Warmsby, Gent.
Richard Clutterbuck, Gent.
Erasmus Smith, Esq.
William Watts, Gent.
John Evelin, Gent.
—— Shapcoate, Gent.
—— Page, Gent.
Thomas Moore, Gent.
Humphery Wray, Gent.
Edward Crafton, Gent.

Alderman Clark.
John Clark, Gent.
Arthur Anneslow.
William Warwick and Purefoy Warwick, Gents.
Captain —— Coape.
Robert Boyle.
Hugh Radcliffe, Gent.
Edward Nelthrop, Gent.
Robert Dixon.
Samuel Clark, Gent.
John Jones, Gent.
Henry Bayne, Gent.
George Clark, Gent.
Edward Hutchinson, Gent.
Richard Aldworth, late Ch. Rememb.
John Briggs, Gent., and John Bucksworth, Esq., all late of the county of Tipperary.
John Kingsmeale of Castlefin, in the county of Donegal, Esq.
James Hamilton of Donmanagh, in the county of Tyrone, Gent.

John Aungier, minister of Lurgan, in the county of Cavan.
Erasmus Smith.
—— Harrison.
Achilles Daunt.
John Power, Lord Decies.
William Gibbs.
Loftus Brightwell.
Robert Beard.
Mathias Aldington.
William Aldington.
John Lovett.
John Castle.
Joseph Ruttorne.
Thomas Valentine.
George Clerk.
John Bright.
George Clerk.
Thomas Chimmicks.
William Warmsby.
Richard Clutterbuck.
Erasmus Smith.
William Watts.
John Evelin.
—— Shapcoate.
—— Page.

Thomas Moore.
Humphery Wray.
Edward Crafton.
Alderman Clerk.
Arthur Anslow.
William Warwick.
Henry Genny, Clerk.
Thomas Assington, Clerk.
Christmas Genny, Clerk.
Thomas Chaplin, Gent.
Archibald Wood, Gent., and John Ball, Gent., all in the county of Ardmagh.
Captain Thomas Smith of Tuam, in the county of Galway.
William Caulfield, Gent.
Edward Eyre, Gent.
Col. Theodore Russel.
Robert Mason, Gent.
Samuel Hudson, Clerk, and Robert Eacelin, Dean of Tuam, all in the county of Galway.
Henry Dowdall of Grange, in the county of Roscommon, Esq.
William Dowdall, Gent.
John French, Esq.

II

TREATY OF LIMERICK
AS RATIFIED BY THEIR MAJESTIES' LETTERS PATENT UNDER
THE GREAT SEAL OF ENGLAND

GULIELMUS ET MARIA, Dei gratia, Angliæ, Scotiæ, Franciæ et Hiberniæ, Rex et Regina, Fidei Defensores, etc. Omnibus ad quos præsentes literæ nostræ pervenerint, salutem; Inspeximus irrotulament. quarund. literarum patentium de confirmatione geren. dat. apud Westmonasterium vicesimo quarto die Februarii ultimi prætoriti in Cancell. nostr. irrotulat. ac ibidem de Record. remanen. in hæc verba.

William and Mary, by the grace of God, etc. To all to whom these presents shall come, greeting: Whereas certain articles bearing date the third day of October last past, made and agreed upon between our Justices of our Kingdom of Ireland and our General of our forces there, on the one part; and several Officers there, commanding within the city of Limerick in our said kingdom, on the other part. Whereby our said Justices and General did undertake that we should ratify those articles within the space of eight months or sooner; and use their utmost endeavours that the same should be ratified and confirmed in Parliament. The tenor of which said articles is as follows:—

Articles agreed upon the third day of October 1691 between the Right Honourable Sir Charles Porter, Knight, and Thomas Coningsby, Esq., Lords Justices of Ireland, and his Excellency the Baron de Ginkell, Lieut. General and Commander in chief of the English army on the one part, and the

Right Honourable Patrick, Earl of Lucan, Percy Viscount Galmoy, Col. Nic. Purcel, Col. Nicholas Cusack, Sir Toby Butler, Col. Dillon, and Col. John Browne, on the other part; in the behalf of the Irish inhabitants in the city and county of Limerick, the counties of Clare, Cork, Kerry, Sligo, and Mayo, in consideration of the surrender of the city of Limerick, and other agreements made between the said Lieut. General Ginkell, the Governor of the city of Limerick, and the Generals of the Irish army, bearing date with these presents, for the surrender of the said city and submission of the said army.

1. The Roman Catholics of this kingdom shall enjoy such privileges in the exercise of their religion as are consistent with the laws of Ireland, or as they did enjoy in the reign of King Charles the Second; and their Majesties, as soon as their affairs will permit them to summon a Parliament in this kingdom, will endeavour to procure the said Roman Catholics such further security in that particular, as may preserve them from any disturbances upon the account of their said religion.

2. All the inhabitants or residents of Limerick, or any other garrison now in the possession of the Irish, and all officers and soldiers now in arms under any commission of King James, or those authorised by him to grant the same, in the several counties of Limerick, Clare, Kerry, Cork, and Mayo, or any of them [and all such as are under their protection in the said counties],[1] and all the commissioned officers in their Majesties' quarters that belong to the Irish regiments now in being, that are treated with, and who are not prisoners of war, or have taken protection, and who shall return and submit to their Majesties' obedience; and their and every of their heirs, shall hold, possess, and enjoy all and every their estates of freehold and inheritance, and all the rights, titles, and interest, privileges and immunities, which they and every, or any of them, held, enjoyed, or were rightfully and lawfully entitled to in the reign of King Charles II, or at any time since by the laws and statutes that were in force in the said reign of King Charles II; and shall be put in possession by order of the Government of such of them as are in the king's hands, or the hands of his tenants, without being put to any suit or trouble therein; and all such estates shall be freed and discharged from all arrears of Crown rents, quit rents, and other public charges incurred and become due since Michaelmas 1688, to the day of the date hereof. And all persons comprehended in this article shall have, hold, and enjoy all their goods and chattels, real and personal, to them or any of them belonging and remaining, either in their own hands, or the hands of any persons whatsoever, in trust for, or for the use of them or any of them; and all and every the said persons, of what profession, trade, or calling soever they be, shall, and may use, exercise, and

---

[1] The words between brackets are the disputed clause, see the ratification at the end. The treaty was signed without this clause.

practise their several and respective professions, trades, and callings, as freely as they did use, exercise, and enjoy the same in the reign of King Charles II. Provided that nothing in this article contained be construed to extend to or restore any forfeiting person now out of the kingdom, except what are hereafter comprised. Provided also, that no person whatsoever shall have or enjoy the benefit of this article, that shall neglect or refuse to take the oath of allegiance, made by the Act of Parliament in England, in the first year of their present Majesties, when thereunto required.[1]

3. All merchants, or reputed merchants of the city of Limerick, or of any other garrison now possessed by the Irish, or of any town or place in the counties of Clare or Kerry, who are absent beyond the seas, that have not borne arms since their Majesties' declaration in February 1688, shall have the benefit of the second article, in the same manner as if they were present; provided such merchants and reputed merchants do repair into this kingdom within the space of eight months from the date hereof.

4. The following officers, viz. Colonel Simon Luttrel, Captain Rowland White, Maurice Eustace of Yermanstown, Chievers of Maystown, commonly called Mount-Leinster, now belonging to the regiments in the aforesaid garrisons and quarters of the Irish army, who were beyond the seas, and sent thither upon affairs of their respective regiments, or the army in general, shall have the benefit and advantage of the second article, provided they return hither within the space of eight months from the date of these presents, and submit to their Majesties' Government, and take the above-mentioned oath.

5. That all and singular the said persons comprised in the second and third articles, shall have the general pardon of all attainders, outlawries, treasons, misprisions of treason, premunires, felonies, trespasses and other crimes and misdemeanours whatsoever by them or any of them committed since the beginning of the reign of James II; and if any of them are attainted by Parliament, the Lords Justices and General will use their best endeavours to get the same repealed by Parliament, and the outlawries to be reversed gratis, all but writing clerks' fees.

6. And whereas these present wars have drawn on great violence on both parts, and that if leave were given to the bringing of all sorts

---

[1] I, A. B., do sincerely promise and swear that I will be faithful and bear true allegiance to their Majesties King William and Queen Mary. So help me God.

of private actions, the animosities would probably continue that have been too long on foot, and the public disturbances last: for the quieting and settling, therefore, of this kingdom, and avoiding those inconveniences which would be the necessary consequence of the contrary, no person or persons whatsoever, comprised in the foregoing articles, shall be sued, molested, or impleaded at the suit of any party or parties whatsoever, for any trespass by them committed, or for any arms, horses, money, goods, chattels, merchandises, or provisions whatsoever, by them seized or taken during the time of the war. And no person or persons whatsoever, in the second or third article comprised, shall be sued, impleaded, or made accountable for the rents or mean rates of any lands, tenements, or houses, by him or them received or enjoyed in this kingdom, since the beginning of the present war to the day of the date hereof, nor for any waste or trespass by him or them committed, in any such lands, tenements, or houses; and it is also agreed that this article shall be mutual and reciprocal on both sides.

7. Every Nobleman and Gentleman comprised in the said second and third article shall have liberty to ride with a sword and case of pistols, if they shall think fit; and keep a gun in their houses for the defence of the same, or for fowling.

8. The inhabitants and residents in the city of Limerick and other garrisons shall be permitted to remove their goods and chattels and provisions out of the same, without being viewed and searched, or paying any manner of duties, and shall not be compelled to leave the houses or lodgings they now have, for the space of six weeks next ensuing the date hereof.

9. The oath to be administered to such Roman Catholics as submit to their Majesties' Government, shall be the oath above said, and no other.

10. No person or persons who shall at any time hereafter break these articles, or any of them, shall thereby make or cause any other person or persons to forfeit or lose the benefit of the same.

11. The Lords Justices and General do promise to use their utmost endeavours that all the persons comprehended in the abovementioned articles shall be protected and defended from all arrests and executions for debt or damage, for the space of eight months next ensuing the date hereof.

12. Lastly, the Lords Justices and the General do undertake that their Majesties will ratify these articles within the space of eight months, or sooner, and use their utmost endeavours that the same shall be ratified and confirmed in Parliament.

13. And whereas Colonel John Brown stood indebted to several Protestants, by judgment of record, which appearing to the late government, the Lord Tyrconnel and Lord Lucan took away the effects of the said John Brown had to answer the said debts, and promised to clear the said John Brown of the said debts; which effects were taken for the public use of the Irish and their army; for freeing the said Lord Lucan of his said engagement, passed on their public account, for payment of the said Protestants, and for preventing the ruin of the said John Brown, and for satisfaction of his creditors, at the instance of the Lord Lucan, and the rest of the persons aforesaid, it is agreed that the said Lords Justices, and the said Baron de Ginckle, shall intercede with the King and Parliament, to have the estates secured to Roman Catholics by articles and capitulation in this kingdom charged with, and equally liable to the payment of so much of the same debts, as the said Lord Lucan, upon stating accounts with the said John Brown, shall certify under his hand, that the effects taken from the said Brown amount unto; which account is to be stated, and the balance certified by the said Lord Lucan, in one and twenty days after the date hereof.

For the true performance hereof, we have hereunto set our hands.

Present, SCRAVENMORE,   CHARLES PORTER,
H. MACKAY,   THOS. CONINGSBY,
T. TALMASH.   Baron de GINCKLE.

And whereas the said city of Limerick hath been since, in pursuance of the said articles, surrendered unto us: Now know you that we, having considered of the said articles, are graciously pleased hereby to declare, that we do for us, our heirs, and successors, as far as in us lies, ratify and confirm the same, and every clause, matter, and thing therein contained. And as to such parts thereof, for which an Act of Parliament shall be found to be necessary, we shall recommend the same to be made good by Parliament, and shall give our royal assent to any bill or bills that shall be passed by our two houses of Parliament to that purpose. And whereas it appears unto us, that it was agreed between the parties to the said articles that after the words, Limerick, Clare, Kerry, Cork, Mayo, or any of them, in the second of the said articles, the words following, viz. "And all such as are under their protection in the said counties," should be inserted and be part of the said articles: Which words having been casually omitted by the writer, the omission was not discovered till after the said articles were signed, but was taken notice of before the second town was surrendered; and that our said justices and general, or one of them, did promise that the said clause should be made good, it being within the intention of the capitulation and inserted in the foul draft thereof: Our further will and pleasure is, and we do hereby ratify and confirm the said omitted words, viz. "And all such as are under their protection in the said counties," hereby for us, our heirs and successors, ordaining and declaring, that all and every person and persons therein concerned shall and may have, receive, and enjoy the benefit thereof in such and the same manner as if the said words had been inserted in their proper place in the said second article, any omission, defect, or mistake in the said second article in any wise notwithstanding. Provided always, and our will and pleasure is, that these our letters patents shall be enrolled in our Court of Chancery in our said kingdom of Ireland within the space of one year next ensuing. IN WITNESS, etc.

MILITARY ARTICLES agreed upon between Lieutenant-General Ginckle, Commander-in-chief of the English army, on one side, and the Lieutenant-Generals D'Usson and De Tesse, Commanders-in-chief of the Irish army, on the other side, and the general officers hereunto subscribing :—

1. That all persons, without any exception, of what quality or condition soever, that are willing to leave the kingdom of Ireland, shall have free liberty to go to any country beyond the seas [England and Scotland excepted] where they think fit, with their families, household stuff, plate, and jewels.

2. That all general officers, colonels, and generally all other officers of horse, dragoons, and foot-guards; troopers, dragoons, soldiers of all kinds that are in any garrison, place, or post, now in the hands of the Irish, or encamped in the counties of Cork, Clare, and Kerry; as also those called rapparees or volunteers, that are willing to go beyond the seas as aforesaid, shall have free leave to embark themselves wherever the ships are that are appointed to transport them, and to come in whole bodies as they are now composed, or in parties, companies, or otherwise, without having any impediment directly or indirectly.

3. That all persons above mentioned, which are willing to leave Ireland and go into France, shall have leave to declare it at the times and places hereafter mentioned, viz. the troops in Limerick on Tuesday next at Limerick; the horse at their camp on Wednesday; and the other forces that are dispersed in the counties of Clare, Kerry, and Cork on the 8th instant, and on none other, before Monsieur Tameron, the French intendant, and Colonel Withers; and after such declaration is made, the troops that will go into France must remain under the command and discipline of their officers that are to conduct them thither; and deserters on each side shall be given up and punished accordingly.

4. That all English and Scotch officers that serve now in Ireland shall be included in this capitulation, as well for the security of their estates and goods in England, Scotland, and Ireland [if they are willing to remain here], as for passing freely into France, or any other country to serve.

5. That all the general French officers, the intendant, the engineers, the commissaries at war, and of the artillery, the treasurer, and other French officers, strangers, and all others whatsoever that are in Sligo, Ross, Clare, or in the army, or that do trade or commerce, or are otherwise employed in any kind of station or condition, shall have free leave to pass into France or any other country, and shall have leave to ship themselves with all their horses, equipage, plate, papers, and all their effects whatever; and that General Ginckle will order transports for them, convoys and carriages, by land and by water, to carry them safe from Limerick to the ships where they shall be embarked, without paying anything for the said carriages, or to those that are employed therein, with their horses, carts, boats, and shallops.

6. That if any of the aforesaid equipages, merchandise, horses, money, plate, or other movables or household stuff belonging to the said Irish troops or to the French officers or other particular persons whatsoever, be robbed, destroyed, or taken away by the troops of the said general, the said general will order it to be restored, or payment to be made according to the value that is given in upon oath by the person so robbed or plundered; and the said Irish troops to be transported as aforesaid, and all persons belonging to them, are to observe good orders in their march and quarters, and shall restore whatever they shall take from the country or make restitution for the same.

7. That to facilitate the transporting the said troops, the general will furnish fifty ships, each ship burthen two hundred tuns, for which the persons to be transported shall not be obliged to pay, and twenty more if there shall be occasion without their paying for them; and if any of the said ships shall be of lesser burthen, he will furnish more in number to countervail, and also give two men-of-war to embark the principal officers and serve for a convoy to the vessels of burthen.

8. That a commissary shall be sent forthwith to Cork to visit the transport ships and see what condition they are in for sailing, and that as soon as they are ready, the troops to be transported shall march with all convenient speed the nearest way in order to embark there; and if there shall be any more men to be transported than can be carried off in the said fifty ships, the rest shall quit the English

town of Limerick and march to such quarters as shall be appointed for them convenient for their transportation, where they shall remain till the other twenty ships are ready, which they are to be in a month, and may embark on any French ships that may come in the mean while.

9. That the said ships shall be furnished with forage for horse, and all necessary provisions to subsist the officers, troopers, dragoons, and soldiers, and all other persons that are shipped to be transported into France; which provision shall be paid for as soon as all are disembarked at Brest or Nantz upon the coast of Brittany or any other part of France they can make.

10. And to secure the return of the said ships [the danger of the seas excepted] and payment for the said provisions, sufficient hostages shall be given.

11. That the garrisons of Clare castle, Ross, and all other foot that are in garrison in the counties of Clare, Cork, and Kerry, shall have the advantage of this present capitulation; and such part of those garrisons as design to go beyond seas shall march out with their arms, baggage, drums beating, ball in mouth, match lighted at both ends, and colours flying, with all provisions, and half the ammunition that is in the said garrisons, and join the horse that march to be transported; or if then there is not shipping enough for the body of foot that is to be next transported after the horse, General Ginckle will order that they be furnished with carriages for that purpose; and what provision they shall want in their march, they paying for the said provisions, or else that they may take it out of their own magazines.

12. That all the troops of horse and dragoons that are in the counties of Cork, Kerry, and Clare, shall also have the benefit of this capitulation; and that such as will pass into France shall have quarters given them in the counties of Clare and Kerry apart from the troops that are commanded by General Ginckle until they be shipped; and within their quarters they shall pay for everything except forage and pasture for their horses which shall be furnished gratis.

13. Those of the garrison of Sligo that are joined to the Irish army shall have the benefit of this capitulation, and orders shall be sent unto them that are to convoy them up to bring them hither to Limerick the shortest way.

14. The Irish may have liberty to transport nine hundred horses, including horses for the officers, which shall be transported gratis;

and as for the troopers that stay behind, they shall dispose of themselves as they shall think fit, giving up their arms and horses to such persons as the general shall appoint.

15. It shall be permitted to those that are appointed to take care for the subsistence of the horse that are willing to go into France, to buy hay and corn at the king's rates wherever they can find it in the quarters that are assigned for them, without any let or molestation; and to carry all necessary provision out of the city of Limerick; and for this purpose the general will furnish convenient carriages for them to the places where they shall be embarked.

16. It shall be lawful to make use of the hay preserved in the stores of the county of Kerry for the horses that shall be embarked; and if there be not enough, it shall be lawful to buy hay and oats where ever they can be found at the king's rates.

17. That all prisoners of war that were in Ireland the 28th of September shall be set at liberty on both sides; and the General promises to use his endeavours that those that are in England or Flanders shall be set at liberty also.

18. The general will cause provisions and medicines to be furnished to the sick and wounded officers, troopers, dragoons, and soldiers of the Irish army that cannot pass into France at the first embarkment; and after they are cured, will order them ships to pass into France if they are willing to go.

19. That at the signing hereof the general will send a ship express to France, and that besides he will furnish two small ships of those that are now in the river of Limerick to transport two persons into France that are to be sent to give notice of this treaty, and that the commanders of the said ships shall have orders to put ashore at the next port in France they shall make.

20. That all those of the said troops, officers or soldiers of what character so ever that will pass into France shall not be stopped on the account of debt or other pretext.

21. If after the signing this present treaty and before the arrival of the fleet, a French packet-boat or other transport-ship shall arrive from France in any part of Ireland, the general will order a passport not only for such as must go on board the said ships, but to the ships to come to the nearest port or place where the troops to be transported shall be quartered.

22. That after the arrival of the fleet there shall be free communication and passage between it and the quarters of the abovesaid troops; and especially for all those that have passes from the

chief commanders of the said fleet or from Monsieur Tameron the intendant.

23. In consideration of the present capitulation the two towns of Limerick shall be delivered and put into the hands of the General, or any other person that he shall appoint, at the times and days hereafter specified, viz. the Irish town, except magazines and hospital, on the day of the signing these present articles; and as for the English town, it shall remain together with the island and free passage of Thomond Bridge in the hands of those of the Irish army that are now in the garrison or that shall hereafter come from the counties of Cork, Clare, Kerry, Sligo, and other places above mentioned, until there shall be conveniency found for their transportation.

24. And to prevent all disorders that may happen between the garrison that the general shall place in the Irish town which shall be delivered to him, and the Irish troops that shall remain in the English town and the island, which they may do until the troops to be embarked on the first fifty ships shall be gone for France, and no longer, they shall intrench themselves on both sides, to hinder the communication of the said garrisons, and it shall be prohibited on both sides to offer any thing that is offensive, and the parties offending shall be punished on either side.

25. That it shall be lawful for the said garrison to march out at once or at different times as they can be embarked, with arms, baggage, drums beating, match lighted at both ends, bullet in mouth, colours flying, six brass guns such as the besieged shall choose, two mortar pieces, and half the ammunition that is now in the magazines of the said place; and for this purpose an inventory of all the ammunition in the garrison shall be made in the presence of any person that the general shall appoint the next day after the present articles be signed.

26. All the magazines of provisions shall remain in the hands of those that are now employed to take care of the same for the subsistence of those of the Irish army that will pass into France; and if there shall not be sufficient in the stores for the support of the said troops while they stay in this kingdom and are crossing the seas, that upon giving an account of their numbers, the general will furnish them with sufficient provisions at the king's rates; and that there shall be a free market in Limerick and other quarters where the said troops shall be. And in case any provisions shall remain in the magazines of Limerick when the town shall be given up, it shall be

valued and the price deducted out of what is to be paid for the provisions to be furnished to the troops on shipboard.

27. That there shall be a cessation of arms at land as also at sea with respect to the ships, whether English, Dutch, or French, designed for the transportation of the said troops until they shall be returned to their respective harbours; and that on both sides they shall be furnished with sufficient passports both for ships and men; and if any sea-commander or captain of a ship, any officer, trooper, dragoon, or soldier, or any other person, shall act contrary to this cessation, the persons so acting shall be punished on either side and satisfaction shall be made for the wrong that is done; and officers shall be sent to the mouth of the river of Limerick to give notice to the commanders of the English and French fleets of the present conjuncture that they may observe the cessation of arms accordingly.

28. That for surety of the execution of this present capitulation and of each article therein contained, the besieged shall give the following hostages.

29. If before this capitulation is fully executed there happens any change in the government or command of the army, which is now commanded by General Ginckle, all those that shall be appointed to command the same, shall be obliged to observe and execute what is specified in these articles, or cause it to be executed punctually, and shall not act contrary on any account.

> D'Usson,
> Le Chevalier de Tesse,
> Latour Montfort,
> Mark Talbot,
> Lucan,
> Jo. Wauchop,
> Galmoy,
> M. Purcell.

THE END

BY THE SAME AUTHOR.

A HISTORY OF THE LEGISLATIVE UNION OF GREAT BRITAIN AND IRELAND.

Demy 8vo. 10s. 6d.

Mr. John **Bright** in his letter to the *Times*, 8th August 1887, says :—" I have read Mr. Dunbar Ingram's book with great interest, and hope it may be widely read. . . . Mr. Ingram's excellent book will be very useful with all who can read and reason upon the great contest which is now before us."

The **Spectator** says :—" With the greatest possible delight we recognise that this task has been fairly undertaken by very competent hands, and that the result is, on the whole, in the highest degree satisfactory. . . . The service which he has rendered to the country at the present time is very great ; and we cannot too strongly urge all those who care to be brought into contact with original authorities, and to have decisive evidence laid before them, to convince themselves how completely baseless most of the charges against Pitt and Castlereagh are. . . . We heartily commend the book to the attention of all those who either care for the honour of English statesmen in the past or who have been affected in the present controversy by the argument that her independence was in 1801 filched from Ireland by the influence of English gold poured into the lap of traitors."

The **St. James's Gazette** says :—" He has dealt with his task with a praiseworthy industry. He never exceeds the scope of his work. His facts are well authenticated, and the conclusions he draws from them are fair and temperate."

The **Scotsman** says :—" His History of the Legislative Union may be recommended as an interesting and valuable discussion of the question ; and Mr. Ingram has the high merit of giving chapter and verse for all his most potent assertions. . . . Nobody can read his book without coming to the conclusion that many of the popular theories respecting the passing of the Union are absolutely devoid of foundation."

The **Guardian** says :—" It is for the most part valuable . . . for its facts, which are admirably full. . . . ' The Union was practically carried in 1799.' There is thus neither good evidence nor good presumption in favour of the wild language with which we are so familiar. Such is the case which Dr. Dunbar Ingram lays before us with great care and skill."

John Bull says :—" Dr. Ingram has done good service in the compilation of ' A History of the Legislative Union of Great Britain and Ireland.' In it he has exposed many popular errors and misconceptions relative to that history. . . . It is most advisable at the present time that the clouds of misrepresentation . . . should be dispelled by the plain statement of facts here put forward, supported as it is by documentary evidence which cannot be shaken."

The **Glasgow Herald** says :—" This is a very able, and, in the present political crisis, a very important work. . . . It is impossible here to follow the chain of evidence which Mr. Ingram has, with painstaking labour, evolved in support of his assertions. It is clear, coherent, and incontestable. He abundantly makes out his case, and is to be complimented upon one of the most valuable additions to the literature of the Irish question."

The **Adelaide Observer** says :—" The book, apart from the question of his partisanship, contains much information which will be welcomed by the ordinary reader who wishes to obtain an insight into the relations which existed between England, afterwards Great Britain, and Ireland prior to 1800."

MACMILLAN AND CO., LONDON.

MESSRS. MACMILLAN AND CO.'S PUBLICATIONS.

Letters on Unionist Delusions. By A. V. DICEY, B.C.L., of the Inner Temple, Barrister-at-Law; Vinerian Professor of English Law; Fellow of All Souls College, Oxford; Hon. LL.D., Glasgow. Crown 8vo. 2s. 6d.

The *Guardian* says:—"Mr. Dicey writes both as a man of letters and as a man of war. He is just the adviser whom the times need. His arguments are those of a quietly reflecting thinker; his counsels are bold and plain.... The book is for its size perhaps the most pregnant we have ever read.... We cannot thank Mr. Dicey enough for the service he has rendered to the Unionist cause by its publication. It ought to form the combative text-book of every combative Unionist."

The *Belfast Northern Whig* says:—"These remarkable letters.... Their publication at the present juncture is opportune, and Professor Dicey's little volume should have a wide circulation."

A NEW BOOK BY MR. JAMES RUSSELL LOWELL.

Political Essays. By JAMES RUSSELL LOWELL, author of "Democracy: and Other Addresses," etc. Extra crown 8vo. 7s. 6d.

The *Academy* says:—"The essays Mr. Lowell has reprinted are important, not alone for their historical interest—which is considerable—but still more because they show us clearly the attitude and the tone of 'the independent in politics' at the time of the great national crisis."

Now publishing, crown 8vo, price 2s. 6d. each.

TWELVE ENGLISH STATESMEN.

The *Times* says:—"We had thought that the cheap issues of uniform volumes on all manner of subjects were being overdone; but the 'Twelve English Statesmen,' published by Messrs. Macmillan, induce us to reconsider that opinion. Without making invidious comparisons, we may say that nothing better of the sort has yet appeared, if we may judge by the five volumes before us. The names of the writers speak for themselves."

William the Conqueror. By EDWARD A. FREEMAN, D.C.L., LL.D. [*Ready.*
Henry II. By Mrs. J. R. GREEN. [*Ready.*
Edward I. By F. YORK POWELL.
Henry VII. By JAMES GAIRDNER.
Cardinal Wolsey. By Professor M. CREIGHTON, M.A., D.C.L., LL.D. [*Ready.*
Elizabeth. By the DEAN OF ST. PAUL'S.
Oliver Cromwell. By FREDERIC HARRISON. [*Ready.*
William III. By H. D. TRAILL. [*Ready.*
Walpole. By JOHN MORLEY. [*In the press.*
Chatham. By JOHN MORLEY. [*Shortly.*
Pitt. By JOHN MORLEY.
Peel. By J. R. THURSFIELD.

The Statesman's Year-Book. A Statistical and Historical Annual of the States of the Civilised World for the year 1887. Twenty-fourth Annual Publication. Revised after Official Returns. Edited by J. SCOTT KELTIE, Librarian to the Royal Geographical Society. Crown 8vo. 10s. 6d.

Annals of Our Time. A Diurnal of Events, Social and Political, Home and Foreign, from the Accession of Queen Victoria to the Peace of Versailles, 28th February 1871. By JOSEPH IRVING. Sixth Edition, revised. 8vo. 18s. Supplements from February 1871 to March 1874. 8vo. 4s. 6d. From March 1874 to July 1878. 8vo. 4s. 6d. From July 1878 down to the Jubilee-Day of Queen Victoria's Reign. [*In the Press.*

How the Peasant Owner Lives in Parts of France, Germany, Italy, and Russia. By Lady VERNEY. Crown 8vo. 5s. 6d.

The *Morning Post* says:—"All who wish for the dissemination of sound ideas calculated to refute the present fallacies advocated by many on the proprietorship of land will welcome Lady Verney's book. In a small space her book offers a large amount of interesting and highly instructive information."

The *Perthshire Advertiser* says:—"Lady Verney's remarks are particularly appropriate at this time when so much is being talked about peasant ownerships in Ireland."

The *Leeds Mercury* says:—"Much may be learned from the book concerning the actual condition of the peasantry in Europe."

Works by the Author of "Hogan, M.P."
Globe 8vo. 2s. each.

Hogan, M.P.	Flitters, Tatters, and the Counsellor;
The Honourable Miss Ferrard.	Weeds; and other Sketches.
Ismay's Children.	Christy Carew.

The *Times* says of *Ismay's Children*:—"Another novel from the pen of the author of *Hogan, M.P.*, and one which can have nothing but commendation.... The series of pictures which it comprises of Irish life and character is full of beauty, humour, and pathos."

The *Guardian* says:—"Amongst the various books which have been written on Ireland it is not too much to say that *Ismay's Children* is one that has depicted most powerfully and accurately the conditions of the Irish peasantry.... The book, as a whole, captivates the imagination and bites itself in the memory."

The *St. James's Gazette* says:—"Read this work [*Ismay's Children*] for an exposition of Irish life, Irish scenery and character, and you will find both entertainment and information."

MACMILLAN AND CO., LONDON.

www.ingramcontent.com/pod-product-compliance
Lightning Source LLC
Chambersburg PA
CBHW030306170426
43202CB00009B/887